YOUR DAYS ARE NUMBERED

YOUR DAYS ARE NUMBERED

A Manual of Numerology for Everybody

BY

FLORENCE CAMPBELL, M.A.

 DeVorss Publications

DeVorss & Company, Publisher
P.O. Box 550
Marina del Rey, CA 90294

Printed in The United States of America

FOREWORD

I've got your number!

When you say that or hear that, don't smile. Your name may be your fortune—or your misfortune. For your name is your number and your number is part of an age-old science.

That science is Numerology.

It is an exact science but a simple one. If you know your own name and can count up to 10, you can discover your own destiny—by simple figures.

It's as easy as that. It's as exact as this:

By taking the numerical value of each letter in your name and adding them by a process of easy arithmetic, you can pick the right jobs, mates, friends, places and times—and you can show yourself how and when to solve each important problem in your life.

Numerology is as old as recorded history. It is also as new as the next decision you are going to make. Where friends advise you, Numerology *directs* you.

It is a science of vibration. Everything moves—up, down, around or across, fast or slow—and it moves at a certain rate—its own. This applies to *you*, to the world around you and to your personal relation to the world, people and things.

We are sure to find our lives at "6's" and "7's" if we attempt to act "1" when the day says "2".

You want to know what to do and what not to do. This book tells you.

CONTENTS

Part I. THE ESSENTIALS

CONTENTS

PART I
THE ESSENTIALS

PART I
THE ESSENTIALS

CHAPTER I

THE VIBRATIONS

In trying to relate ourselves to life as we find it, we must discover how to play harmonies instead of discords. The piano, for example, stands in the living room, capable of many varieties of sounds and noises. If we do not understand how to play it, perhaps it will remain silent until some one comes along who does; if we make the attempt without any understanding, the attempt is likely to be disastrous to ears and nerves.

Why not learn what will produce the harmonies?

We are all equally capable of harmonies and discords but, unlike other manufactured instruments, we may not remain mute and inexpressive. We must take our place in the Cosmic Orchestra. If we are to find full expression in living we must learn how to bring out the harmonies of the inner self.

The clue to this we find in the world around us, for if we pause long enough to sense and *feel* it we discover: Vibration.

The world travels at a rapid rate. Indeed, it has been noted recently by our great scientists that the vibration of the earth is increasing at the rate of one hour a week! If we are not to fall by the wayside, we must vibrate at an equal pace, and the only way to do this is to work *with* the vibrations rather than *against* them, taking our place

I

in their midst and travelling at the rate that belongs to each one of us *individually*.

What Vibrations Mean To You

We are *all* affected by the vibrations that govern the Universe for we are all a part of it. As a part of the whole we are affected by every change in the Universal *rate* of vibration—and the rate changes every time there appears a different *number* in year, month or day. But because we are individuals we also have a rate of our own. So we must consider Universal Year and *Personal* Year; Universal Month and *Personal* Month; Universal Day and *Personal* Day.

The Universal Vibration is like a stage set for a play. We may *read* the whole play but we *memorize* only the lines in our own rôle. If we miss our cues or step out of our character, we are bad actors and have lost our chance.

Finding your own number gives you the chance to take your place in the world and keep it.

The vibrations that belong to the *individual* that is YOU are much more personal and vital than those of your years, months and days. They are determined by your given name *at birth* and the day, month and year when you were born. That is why no two people are ever exactly alike; you may be given a name like your father's or mother's, but your birth date will not be the same; or you may be born on the same day as your twin brother or sister, but you will have a different name. Each letter has its own number; each number has its own meaning.

You have three main influences that vitally affect you. These give you (1) certain urges and desires, (2) certain types of expression and (3) a certain environment and opportunity which you carry through life. Some of these cannot be changed; some can. Every one has a job in life —one that he *wants* to do, is *able* to do or is *obliged* to do —as the case may be. We may want to do something for which we are not fitted; if we insist upon doing it, we can't make a success of it. Or we may feel capable of doing something for which we never find the opportunity. For a variety of reasons, many people are ill-fitted for the kind of work they are engaged in; they are unhappy or dissatisfied with their lot and know no way to improve it. Your numbers will tell you how to adjust yourself to the things that cannot be changed or, by making the changes that are within your power, will attract to you the things you need to help you.

These three main influences in your life are (1) the Soul Urge, (2) the Expression, and (3) the Life Path. The birthday number is also *very* important, but that is a part of the Life Path, so really belongs in the main three.

The *Soul Urge,* or Ideality, is the number of your heart's desire—that which you would like best to do (or that your best self would like to have you do). It is the *motive* that lies behind your acts; the feeling and inclination you put into the day's work; your attitude toward things and people; your judgment, your principles and point of view. This is the great HOW that answers every move you make and every thought you have.

The *Expression* is the sum of your natural capacities and capabilities—that which you most easily *express* because of the vibrations of all the letters of your original name. Here are included your talents and possibilities and here is shown the type of work in which you would feel the most comfortable and the most at home. If the sum of *all* your letters, your final Expression Number, is in harmony with your Soul Urge and your birthdate, you will have little difficulty in choosing your true vocation in life. In any event, it shows you what "tools" you have to work with and is the natural, spontaneous You. For this reason it is usually your *Im*pression as well as your *Ex*pression, for we are judged by what we do rather than by what we are. Your Expression is the WHAT of your life.

These two influences—Soul Urge and Expression—are found from your name, and sometimes they are at odds with each other. What you *want* to do may not fit what you *are* doing and there seems to be constant interference in your life. If that is so, *change your name* to fit your needs and opportunities and draw to yourself new influences that pull with you instead of against you. Your inner self will not be changed—for it cannot—but the new influences will give you external and material help.

The *Life Path* is found from the birthdate. It is the sum of the month, day and year in which you came into life. This is something you cannot change and shows the direction you *must* take, whether you will or not. Here are to be found your opportunities (and the *only* ones you will have) to do the job you are fitted for; here you will meet the people, places and environment that are given you to use to your own advantage. This is the WHERE of your life. Since this is fixed and immovable, we must be careful to choose the kind of work for which the Path will give the opportunity, and we must also be careful to attract to this Path no vibrations of our own choosing that will fail to harmonize. It would be folly, then, to change your name carelessly, or from passing whim or fancy, for you may be attracting to yourself just the things you want to avoid—and your Path of Destiny may not give you any chance to use them.

If you want to change your name, study Numerology or consult some one who is well acquainted with it. The Path gives us a new lesson to learn, a new "initiation" to take and we must bring to it the best we have in order to get from it the chance we need.

The Three Aspects of Each Number

Discovering the meaning of each number is the first important step in Numerology.

Each number has three aspects or "degrees of comparison," such as "good, better, best," or "bad, worse, worst." These three aspects we call

(1) The Constructive
(2) The Negative
(3) The Destructive.

We are *given* the numbers; we *choose* the aspect.

Our numbers have the power to help us if we *choose* to live *constructive* lives. They show their negative side if we slump or drift through life, refusing to do our share of the work. They become destructive when we deliberately take action in the wrong direction.

The majority of people are making honest, *constructive* efforts—or at least they mean to, but the best of us occasionally drift into negativity and it takes unceasing watchfulness to keep away from it. Continued negativity encourages the easy slide downhill and at the bottom of the hill is Destruction. Since we must all obey the Law of Gravity, we must make an effort to keep *up* if we are not to be pulled *down*.

Work out your own Numerological Chart and then examine each one of your numbers in all its aspects. Watch especially the "Negative" column (most of the "Destructives" are behind the bars or so plainly labeled that we easily recognize them) and honestly admit your own faults or backslidings. If you find yourself veering toward the negative you may know you are getting away from the positive, and the negative qualities of your number will pull you still further away. Pull yourself up quickly. You are on the way to becoming an unobtrusive, passive mouse (who will eventually fall into a trap) or a door-mat for the muddy shoes of other people. The vast army of "negatives" are the rut-workers, drudges or parasites—too lazy or too self-satisfied to make any contribution to life. They believe the world owes them a living.

Below are the Numbers in their three aspects. When you have found your own Soul Urge, Expression and Life Path you can see, by consulting this list, your possibilities of attainment in the Constructive aspect, your pitfalls in the Negative and the results that are attained by those benighted individuals who choose the Destructive.

THE THREE ASPECTS OF EACH NUMBER

NUMBER ONE

Constructive:

Creation, Originality, Independence, Courage, Progress, Ambition, Positiveness, Will Power, Leadership, Pioneering, Activity, Force.

Negative:

Laziness, Imitation, Dependence, Selfishness, Instability, Egotism, Weakness, Fear, Braggadocio, Contrariness, Stagnation, Stubbornness.

Destructive:

Tyranny, Monomania, Iconoclasm, Antagonism, Bullying, SELF—at—all—costs.

NUMBER TWO

Constructive:

Love, Service, Gentleness, Harmony, Adaptability, Charm, Diplomacy, Friendliness, Rhythm, Music, Receptivity, Cooperation, Consideration for others.

Negative:

Vacillation, Apathy, Indifference, Shyness, Self-effacement, Over-sensitiveness, Spinelessness, Bootlicking, Sulkiness, Discontent, Slackness, Carelessness.

Destructive:

Deception, Mischief-making, Sullenness, Cruelty, Cowardice, Bad Temper, Slyness, Lying, Pessimism.

NUMBER THREE

Constructive:

Artistic Expression, The Joy of Living, Freedom from Worry, Optimism, Inspiration, Talent, Imagination, Good Taste, Sociability, Friendliness, Kindness.

Negative:

Dilettantism, Worry, Whining, Criticism, Gossip, Extravagance, Vanity, Triviality, Superficiality, Exaggeration, Silly Pride.

Destructive:

Jealousy, Hypocrisy, Wastefulness, Yellow Streak, Intolerance.

NUMBER FOUR

Constructive:

Practicality, Service, Patience, Exactitude, Organization, Application, Devotion, Patriotism, Conservatism, Pragmatism, Dignity, Economy, Trust, Worthiness, Endurance, Loyalty.

Negative:

Plodding, Narrowness, Exaction, Repression, Minuteness, Penuriousness, Clumsiness, Dogmatism, Crudeness, Brusqueness, Restriction, Rigidity, Sternness, Dullness.

Destructive:

Vulgarity, Animalism, Hatred, Violence, Jealousy, Inhumanity, Resistance, Destruction, Cruelty.

NUMBER FIVE

Constructive:

Freedom, Progress, Versatility, Understanding, Variety, Adaptability, Mental curiosity, Life experience, Cleverness, Unattachment, Sociability, Change, Discard, Travel, Adventure, Companionability.

Negative:

Irresponsibility, Procrastination, Carelessness, Self-indulgence, Thoughtlessness, Inconsistency, Sensationalism, Bad Taste.

Destructive:

Libertinism, Perversion, Abuse of freedom, Indulgence in drink, Indulgence in dope, Sensuality.

NUMBER SIX

Constructive:

Love, Harmony, Home, Responsibility, Adjustment, Musical talent, Sympathy, Understanding, Domesticity, Guardianship, Stability, Poise, Protection, Healing, Firmness, Balance, Idealism, Conscientiousness, Justice, Burden-bearing, Service to mankind.

Negative:

Anxiety, Worry, Meddlesomeness, Bustling activity, Misplaced sympathy, Mistaken ideals, Interference, Conventionality, Pride, Smugness, Unwilling service, Drudgery, Despondency.

Destructive:

Cynicism, Egotism, Suspicion, Jealousy, Slavery, Domestic tyranny.

NUMBER SEVEN

Constructive:

Mental analysis, Technicality, Introspection, Peace, Poise, Scientific research, Spirituality, Faith, Trust, Stoicism, Refinement, Wisdom, Silence, "Theories and Fundamentals."

Negative:

Melancholy, Fault-finding, Sarcasm, Coldness, Aloofness, Skepticism, Confusion, Humiliation, Nervousness, Erraticism.

Destructive:

Faithlessness, Turbulence, Drink, Malice, Suppression, Deceitfulness, Theft, Cheating, Craftiness.

NUMBER EIGHT

Constructive:

Power, Authority, Success, Material freedom, Judgment, Discrimination, Executive ability, Organization, Leadership, Management, Practicality, Thoroughness, Dependability, Self-reliance, Control, the Power to *succeed.*

Negative:

Strain, Hardness, Materiality, Ambition for self and money, Demand for recognition, Intolerance, Worry, Scheming, Love of power, Carelessness, Impatience, Poor judgment, Misspent energy.

Destructive:

Bullying, Abuse, Revenge, Oppressiveness, Injustice, Cruelty, Unscrupulousness.

NUMBER NINE

Constructive:

Universal Love, Brotherhood, Charity, Compassion, The Higher Law, Artistic genius, Selfless service, Philanthropy, Humanitarianism, Magnetism, Sympathy, Understanding, Romance, Generosity, Breadth of viewpoint.

Negative:

Emotionalism, Amativeness, Egocentricity, Sentimentality, Dissipation of forces, Indiscretion, Impracticality, Fickleness, Aimless dreaming.

Destructive:

Dissipation, Immorality, Vulgarity, Bitterness, Moroseness.

NUMBER ELEVEN

Constructive:

Intuition, Revelation, Invention, Poetry, Art, Spirituality, Fire, Zeal, Idealism, Priestliness, Evangelism, Martyrdom, Exhortation, Immateriality.

Negative:

Aimlessness, Penuriousness, Shiftlessness, Lack of understanding, Fanaticism, Self-superiority, Imposition of the personal will or standards. (See the Negative 2.)

Destructive:

Miserliness, Debauchery, Degradation, Dishonesty, Deviltry, the attributes of the Crook.

NUMBER TWENTY-TWO

Constructive:

   Power (on all planes), Practical idealism, Direction (international), Uplift (universal), the Material Master.

Negative:

   Promotion (get-rich-quick schemes), "Big Talk," Inferiority complex, Grudging service. (See the Negative 4.) Indifference.

Destructive:

   Viciousness, Black Magic, Crime.

1—9, 11 and 22

Every number may be included in the range from 1 to 9. 9 is the Cycle of Man, who is the "Little Universe," for from 1 to 9 are included all the experiences of which man is capable. 9 Solar months are necessary for life before birth; 9 is the square (man) of the Trinity (God); the sciences reduce themselves to 9 terms; the arts are governed by 9 Muses; language divides itself into 9 grammatical parts. If 9 be added to any number, the number (reduced to a single digit) remains unchanged; if 9 be subtracted from any number greater than itself, the number of the result is the *original* number (reduced to a single digit).

$9 + 5 = 14$, and $1 + 4 = 5$.

$25 - 9 = 16$. If 25 be reduced to a single digit $(2 + 5 = 7)$ the result is 7; if 16 be reduced to a single digit $(1 + 6 = 7)$ the result is 7. In either case, 9 remains untouched and is complete or *perfect* as regards the ordinary computations of man.

10 (reduced) is again 1 — but on a higher "plane" because it marks the return to the Unity from which all things sprang. In Numerology we *reduce* 10 to 1 but *remember* that it is 10 and not *simply* 1.

There are two numbers, however, beyond the cycle of 9, that are not reduced in Numerology and these two are 11 and 22. These are called the MASTER NUMBERS and do not belong on their lower levels of 2 (1 + 1) and 4 (2 + 2). Those who have these Master Numbers in their name or birthdate may know that they are endowed with qualities of leadership and inspiration that are not given to the majority.

The mission of these two numbers, each from its own angle, is selfless service to mankind. They are given only to the "old souls" whose experiences have fitted them to be leaders and masters. They are numbers of high tension and great power, difficult to live up to because of their strict requirements.

11 is the mystic, the dreamer, the impractical visionary. He lives in the clouds and gets his ideals and visions from the higher planes. He is usually clairaudient and clairvoyant (although not always aware of it). It is within his power to give to the world a revelation—for which he may or may not receive his reward on earth. If he seeks nothing for himself and pledges his life to the service of mankind, he is likely to achieve great fame, for the 11 vibration is electrical and broadcasting; if he seeks the platform for his own glorification, he is likely to be struck by his own lightning. 11 usually has little regard for time, place or appointments for he lives in the clouds where those things respond to a different rhythm from our own. 11 is too impractical for an every-day companion,

but he is a Master for he is the messenger and spokesman of the gods.

22 is the *practical* idealist who has seen the vision of 11 and has the power to put it to practical, tangible *use*—for the benefit of mankind. He is the Material Master, who conceives tremendous plans and achieves tremendous results. Owing to the rapid vibration of both of these numbers, they have been known to cause insanity in those not sufficiently balanced to handle them.

Never reduce 11 and 22 when they appear as a final result of your Soul Urge, Expression or Life Path. When they fall *behind* these final results and form a *part* of the total, never lose sight of their presence or disregard their qualities, but add their separate digits only for convenience and *read* them into the final number.

GENERAL CLASSIFICATION OF THE NUMBERS

THE ONE			THE MANY				THE ALL			
1	2	3	4	5	6	7	8	9	11	22
A	B	C	D	E	F	G	H	I	K	V
J		L	M	N	O	P	Q	R		
S	T	U		W	X	Y	Z			

Those who have the majority of numbers in the "One" have come for the purpose of individualization, creation, pioneering, *self*-expression and *self*-development. They are "separatists" and often self-centered. Their Watchword is—MINE.

Those who have the majority in the "Many" include their own family, community and country. They work *with* the masses and are not separated from them. They have a sense of responsibility that extends beyond themselves. Their Watchword is—OURS. 7, although separating himself from the world of form, is still concerned with

the "Many" in connection with "Theories and Fundamentals"—but 7 remains the Bridge Between.

Those in the "All" love humanity *first*, and then the
family and community more impersonally. They make no
distinctions of race or, creed, but serve and live for the
good of all. Their Watchword is—YOURS.

CHAPTER II

HOW TO FIND YOUR SOUL URGE

Vowels are the "Soul of the Language." The vowels in your name give the vibration of your own Soul Urge.*

To find the number value of each letter, consult the following Table.

1	2	3	4	5	6	7	8	9
A	B	C	D	E	F	G	H	I
J	[K]	L	M	N	O	P	Q	R
S	T	U	[V]	W	X	Y	Z	

Note: K, the *11*th letter of the alphabet, and V, the *22*nd letter, have the value of 11 and 22 respectively.

These are the Master Numbers and are left unreduced.

Vowels

Every syllable must contain a vowel.

The principal vowels are A E I O U.

W is a vowel only when united to another vowel and sounded as one—(as AW, EW, OW).

---

* Mrs. L. Dow Balliett, the first teacher of Numerology in the Western world, made the valuable contribution of adding the *vowels* of the name, apart from the consonants, to discover the vibration of the Soul.

Y is a vowel (1) When preceded by another vowel and sounded as one—(as AY, EY, OY) and (2) When there is no other vowel in the syllable.

All numbers (except 11 and 22) are reduced to a final digit by adding them together until a *single* number remains.

For example:—We set up the full name of Amelia Clare Bronn, and *above* each *vowel* place its number value, as found in the Table.

```
1   5   9 1       1   5   6
A M E L I A   C L A R E  B R O N N
```

Adding together the vowels of AMELIA, we have, as a result, 16.
Reducing 16 to its final digit (1+6=7)............................ 7
Adding together the vowels of CLARE (1+5=6).................. 6
Adding together the vowels of BRONN (6)....................... 6
                                                              ——
The sum of these three is.....................................19
    Reducing 19 to its final digit (1+9=10, =1) we find that the vowel-sum, or Soul Urge of AMELIA CLARE BRONN is 1.

For the meaning of 1 as a Soul Urge, consult the Table of the Soul Urge.

Find your own Soul Urge or that of any of your friends in the same manner, being careful to use *all* the names that were given *at birth,* for only from the full name that you *started* with can you find your true Soul Urge.

Later on you will want to know just what *kind* of a final digit you have—that is, what there is *behind* it. For that you will look at the sum of each name separately. The *kind* of a 19 or 1 in the Soul of Amelia Clare Bronn is a 7-6-6. She *might* have had a 19 or 1 Soul Urge made up of 9-9-1, or 6-8-5 or many other combinations; but *her* 19 or 1 is 7-6-6 *because* the vowels of her separate names total to 7, 6 and 6. With a different name she might have had a 19 or 1 Soul Urge, but it would have been a slightly different kind of a 19 or 1.

Until you are familiar with the meanings of the numbers, consider only the final digits—the rest will come easily later. You will be surprised to find how much your numbers will tell you about yourself—what you already know, what you only half suspected and what you have always hoped was true.

Table of the Soul Urge

Number 1

Wants to lead and direct. Refers everything to himself. Prefers to work alone or with subordinates.

Is proud of his abilities and wants to be praised for them.

Seeks opportunities to display his strength and usefulness.

Wants to create and originate.

Wants to handle only the main issues—leaving the details to others.

Wants "my wife," "my children," "my home" to be a credit to him.

Wants to dominate any situation in which he finds himself.

Is not very emotional and love is not necessary to his happiness.

Is capable of great accomplishment.

Is loyal in friendship, strictly fair in business—a safe leader.

May be rather boastful and egotistic, critical, impatient of trifles.

> All 1's need to cultivate—
> Friendliness and Human Interest.

Number 2

Wants (and needs) love, society and companionship.

Wants to work for others—and with them.

Wants harmony and peace.

Does not object to obscurity.

Wants ease and comfort, but does not demand wealth and luxury.

Is not ambitious and does not insist upon his rights or viewpoint.

Is kind and thoughtful of others.

Is a natural peacemaker and diplomat.

Attracts hosts of friends—even those who are mutual enemies.

Can keep all secrets—his own and others.

Is not over-frank for fear of causing unhappiness.

Is very sensitive and emotional.

Falls in love easily and cries frequently.

Is devoted, indulgent, "soft."

Is not given to disciplining himself or others.

Is easy-going, harmonious, friendly.

Loves all things rhythmic and musical.

Has no regard for exactitude or rigidity.

Is contented with small things.

Is often studious, *accumulating* much wisdom.

Attracts many things to himself and absorbs them easily

> All 2's need to cultivate—
> Strength of Purpose and Definiteness.

NUMBER 3

Wants to give out joy and happiness.

Wants to scatter his love, activities, energy and talents broadcast.

Wants popularity and many friends.

Wants beauty in all his surroundings.

Never worries or allows depression to get the upper hand.

Takes life as it comes and laughs at discouragement or failure.

Refers everything to the heart-side of life—but never tragically.

Never mopes over mistakes in marriage, love or business; tries again.

Never asks for more than he finds.

Is always interested and entertained.

Is always artistic and expressive.

Loves to entertain and give everyone a good time.

Loves children, pets and all animals.

Loves to flirt but is usually not unfaithful.

Makes a game out of life.

> All 3's need to cultivate—
> Concentration and Patience.

NUMBER 4

Wants respectability and solidity.

Wants to serve and be a rock of dependability.

Is willing to deny himself that others may benefit.

Is a great disciplinarian—for himself and others.

Loves home, family and country.

Wants his work cut out for him—and will do exactly as
he is told.

Bows to his superior, his own conscience and tradition.

Is not fond of innovations.

Loves order and regularity.

Is constant, faithful, dependable.

Needs and wants much love, but often repels it by his
own austerity.

Hates pretension and insincerity.

Is thorough and methodical.

Has great pride of family and the conventions.

> All 4's need to cultivate—
> Breadth of Viewpoint and Discard of the Outworn.

NUMBER 5

Wants personal freedom in every direction.

Wants change, variety and constant new opportunity.

Wants to learn about life in all its phases.

Will not be hampered by convention or the ideas of
others.

Loves pleasure, travel, sports, art, science, music, languages.

Hates to wait and hates to stick.

Cannot submit to routine or detail.

Loves strange and new people, places and things.

Is progressive, intellectual, emotional, versatile—often
spiritual.

Adapts himself to any condition, country or class of
people.

Injects new life into all that he touches—then passes
quickly on.

Needs many and varied interests, sunshine and crowds.
Discards readily and holds to nothing.
Takes responsibility lightly—or not at all.

>All 5's need to cultivate—
>Loyalty, Patience and Steadiness of Purpose.

Number 6

Wants responsibility, steadfast love, home, domesticity,
    roots.
Is a good counsellor and loyal friend.
Is a refuge and asylum for those in need of comfort or
    shelter.
Is inclined toward conventionality, but is broad-minded
    and sympathetic.
Loves ease, comfort, beauty, music and harmony.
Is artistic, kind and understanding.
Has no ambition to make a great name, but is usually
    well protected.
Wants to right and adjust all wrongs—and everybody's
    life.
Is a sort of cosmic parent or guardian.
Originated the saying, "There ought to be a law," etc.
Is a fine judge of character when the emotions are not
    too involved.
Centers his life about his home and loved ones.
Loves to work with others—never alone.
Likes praise and thanks, but gives willing service.

>All 6's need to cultivate—
>Firmness and Assertiveness to balance their
>Emotions and Judgment; a less *Personal* Attitude.

NUMBER 7

Wants silence and peace to live his inner life.

Wants to meditate upon his dreams of perfection.

Hates the noise and confusion of the business world.

Is seldom understood because so withdrawn and alone.

Hates the new, sudden or ephemeral.

Loves old gardens, pictures, furniture—mellowed by time.

Hates to soil his hands or closely contact the realities of life.

Loves to analyze, dissect, examine and consider from every angle.

Goes to the *roots* of all things and demands the "reason why."

Loves to be alone but fears loneliness and poverty.

Is conservative, refined, reserved, spiritual.

Is sought for his wisdom but does not shine in society.

Is innately shy and has no "casual conversation."

Is deeply emotional but has a horror of showing it.

Subjects all things to keen mental analysis.

Wants each detail perfected before passing on to the next.

Is a well of secrecy.

Is intellectual, scientific, philosophical—or meta-philosophical.

Must be *known* to be loved.

> All 7's need to cultivate—
> Understanding and Sympathy,
> The Avoidance of Fear and Melancholy.
> They must learn to be
> "Alone and not lonely."

NUMBER 8

Wants big affairs and the power to handle them.
Wants success in all material matters.
Loves organization, construction, finances.
Loves the huge operations of the commercial world.
Loves to manage and direct.
Has the ability for great achievement and accumulation.
Is generous, large-minded, powerful and dependable.
Has strength, enthusiasm, courage, poise and determination.
Loves to struggle against opposition—confident of his victory.
May be dominant and exacting, but never spares himself.
May be fond of money and display but is a Cornerstone of the Community.
Has vision and imagination for making his efforts pay.
Is efficient, executive and of excellent judgment.
Is a power for good.

> All 8's need to cultivate—
> Justice and Toleration for the weaker and less efficient.

NUMBER 9

Wants to serve the whole world.
Wants to give to all the benefits of his knowledge and experience.
Is the interpreter of the greatness to be found in life.
Is the Great Lover.
Gives of himself without thought of his own impoverishment.
Has boundless faith in his own source of supply.

Is the Universal Brother—sympathetic, understanding, serving.

Has wisdom, intuition, broadness of mind and viewpoint.

Wants personal love, but *belongs* to the Universe.

Suffers through his emotions and elimination of personality.

Is attractive to all and loved by all.

Is ready to give his life for humanity.

Is a great artist and wants his message to benefit the world.

Wants to "broadcast" himself, his talents, his emotions.

All 9's need to cultivate—
Definiteness, Balance, Emotional Control.

NUMBER 11

Wants to reveal the beauties he has seen and known.

Wants to preach the necessity of living true to ideals.

Wants all men to know *his* idea of God.

Wants to indulge in impracticality, but seem practical.

Provides universal remedies but does not understand human needs.

Is always the universalist—never concerned with individuals.

Is a dreamer and visionary, with a passion for salvation and uplift.

Loves his ideals rather than his fellow-man.

Insists upon *right*—as he sees it—regardless of the human equation.

Has great interior strength and the devotion of the martyr.

Wants to choose his friends from among his own kind.
Has an "electrical" type of mind and is capable of remarkable inventions.

> All 11's need to cultivate—
> Human Understanding.

NUMBER 22

Wants to be the *perfect* builder—for the good and security
of all.
Loves Form, but wants it perfectly constructed, for *use*.
Realizes the necessity for practicality in a practical world.
Is POWER to the nth degree and Master of every situa-
tion.
Is respected and looked up to and never betrays a con-
fidence.
Stands for the ideal realized.
Is the true Master-Builder—building for eternity.
Has his eyes on the stars but his feet on the ground.
Has the leadership of 1, the kindness of 2, the imagina-
tion of 3, the patience of 4, the freedom and progress
of 5, the balance of 6, the spirituality of 7, the
executive power of 8, the love of humanity of 9, the
vision of 11—*united* in his super-human 22.

> All 22's need to cultivate—
> The Steadfast Adherence to their Ideals
> in the midst of materiality.

CHAPTER III

YOUR LATENT OR QUIESCENT SELF

WHAT YOU ARE EXPRESSING

Your latent or quiescent self is your *consonant* sum. This number is quiescent because not active in your daily life. Your vowels are always active in your Soul; your vowels and consonants *together* are active in your Expression; your consonants are active only in the individual letters, but their *sum* is you *at rest*.

Your consonant number is your own secret for it is *you* devoid of the necessity for aspiration or ambition, *you* when you are alone, concerned only with your own dreams, relieved from responding to outside influences. As soon as another person or idea enters your atmosphere you have a reaction, and are no longer quiescent or wholly "consonantal."

As an example of how to find the Quiescent Self, we again set up the name of AMELIA CLARE BRONN, and *under* each consonant place its number value:

```
A M E L I A   C L A R E   B R O N N
  4   3         3 3   9    2 9   5 5
```

7	+	(15)	6	+	(21)	3	=16, =7

Adding together the consonants of AMELIA, we have...... 7
Adding together the consonants of CLARE, we have....... 6
Adding together the consonants of BRONN, we have....... 3

The sum of these three is..............................16
Reducing 16 to a final digit (1+6=7) we find that the consonant-sum or Quiescent Self of Amelia Clare Bronn is 7.

Find your own Quiescent Self by the same process, then consult the following Table for your own number and see if that does not represent what you really dream about when nobody is watching you.

TABLE OF THE QUIESCENT SELF

NUMBER 1

Courageous, daring. Dreaming of fields as yet unconquered, heights as yet unattained, shores as yet untouched. You picture yourself as the leader, instigator and promoter of new plans and enterprises hitherto unconceived.

NUMBER 2

Protected, loved, comforted. Surrounded by those you care for. You see home and children, an atmosphere of peace and harmony, with yourself in the background, quietly serving and ministering to the comfort of all in little, unobtrusive ways.

NUMBER 3

Your imagination pictures you as popular, attractive and sought after. You always have an appreciative audience and all your sayings and doings are applauded. You see yourself expressing in art-forms, shedding beauty and happiness wherever you go.

NUMBER 4

You are the pillar of society upon whom all depend. You see yourself working tirelessly for the rewards of accomplishment, duty, love and appreciation. You are the staunch patriot who is recognized as the savior of his country.

NUMBER 5

You are free to travel to all the countries of the world, unhampered by ties or responsibilities. You see yourself conversing fluently in all tongues, mingling with the natives of many foreign lands, living for adventure and life experience.

NUMBER 6

You are the center of an adoring family. You have a beautiful, artistic home and keep its hospitable gates wide open. You have flowers and music around you and love the responsibility of running a perfectly ordered menage. Your picture of the future is yourself and your lover walking arm in arm in your lovely garden or, hand in hand, with white heads close together, sitting by your own fireside. Your "higher 6" causes you to see yourself as the Cosmic comforter and adjuster.

NUMBER 7

You see yourself in a beautiful library full of rare books, choice pictures and old furniture. Your windows look out on peaceful low hills and your own garden in full bloom. Many come to you to learn wisdom from your lips, but much of your time is spent alone in quiet meditation. You usually wear a long robe, beautifully embroidered with the symbols that mean much to you. You are the Priest and Mystic whose mind is stored with the wisdom of the Ancients.

Number 8

You are on many Boards of Directors and the President of many banks and companies. Your suite of offices is richly furnished and your staff of employees very large. You conduct your business on an enormous scale and deal in international affairs.

Number 9

You are one of the world's great artists. You are filled with a love for humanity and are eager to be of service— no matter at what cost to yourself. You long for personal love and happiness, but realize that your mission is impersonal service and that therein lies your only chance for happiness. Highly emotional yourself, you understand the sufferings of others and many come to you for comfort and advice. You see yourself as a spectator, looking down on the struggles and mistakes that you have overcome.

Number 11

You are one of the messengers who is to "go into all the world and preach the gospel to every creature." The light of divine fire is in your eyes and through your inspired exhortations you are able to guide many to the Truth as you see it. You would die for your faith and glory in your martyrdom.

Number 22

You dream of the union of all nations and countries in constructive activity. You plan great waterways and railroad systems that shall speed up commerce and international intercourse. You dream of ways and means that

shall make the earth yield her treasures for the benefit
of all. You build great factories which are models of
beauty, marvels of efficiency and a joy to those who are
privileged to work in them. Your dreams take *form*.

WHAT YOU ARE EXPRESSING

Your Expression is found from the sum of *all* the letters
of your given name—the Essence of the vibrations that
make up the grand total of YOU.

To discover this, we set up the full given name and
place the number value *beneath* each letter.

For example, we again set up the name of Amelia Clare
Bronn, this time putting vowels and consonants together
under the name:—

A M E L I A	C L A R E	B R O N N	
1 4 5 3 9 1	3 3 1 9 5	2 9 6 5 5	
(23=) 5 +	(21=) 3 +	(27=) 9	=17,=8

We have figured the total of each name separately and
reduced each total to a final digit—then reduced the
sum of the totals to a final digit, which we find to be 8—
the Expression number of Amelia Clare Bronn.

We are now ready to set up her Table completely, sum-
ming the Vowels (Soul Urge), the Consonants (Quiescent
Self) and the Total (Expression).*

By frequently referring to the Table of the "Three
Aspects" in Chapter 1, you will soon learn to recognize

---

* *Never* figure the Expression from the sum of the Soul Urge and
Quiescent Self; *always* use the third process of setting up the numbers
of all the letters in a separate line. By resorting to the shorter method
you are likely to lose an 11 or 22 or to find one that doesn't belong
to the Expression.

(16) 7	+	6	+	6	= 19, = 1 *Soul Urge*

1 5 9 1	1 5	6
A M E L I A	C L A R E	B R O N N
4 3	3 3 9	2 9 5 5

7	+	(15) 6	+	(21) 3	= 16, = 7 Quiescent Self

1 4 5 3 9 1	3 3 1 9 5	2 9 6 5 5

(23) 5	+	(21) 3	+	(27) 9	= 17, = 8 *Expression*

the *general* meaning of each number. Each number, however, has also a *specific* meaning according to its location in the Chart—as Soul Urge, Quiescent Self, Expression or Life Path, and for that reason there is a separate Table for each division.

We are always interested to know whether the majority of our numbers are odd or even, for this gives us still more information about ourselves. The odd numbers (1, 3, 5, 7, 9, 11) are inspirational and artistic. The even numbers (2, 4, 6, 8, 22) create in *form*. The numbers 1, 6 and 22 are "dual," for they are inspirational artists *within*, but capable of expression in form *without*.

You may have a mixture of both, so look behind the *final* numbers of Soul Urge and Expression, at the digits of your *separate* names and see which you have the most of. The *final* number is the most important.

THE GREAT WITHIN	THE GREAT WITHOUT *
1, 3, 5, 7, 9, 11	2, 4, 6, 8, 22

"DUAL"—1, 6, 22

The "Withins" test all things subjectively and emotionally; their vision is broad and idealistic; they love art,

* Classification by Dr. Seton.

beauty and spirituality. DREAMERS. They strive for Illumination.

The "Withouts" test all things objectively, for use and efficiency; they are concerned with construction, activity and material power. DOERS. They strive for Success.

TABLE OF THE EXPRESSION

NUMBER 1

Pioneer or explorer.

Creator or originator; Inventor.

Leader, director, manager.

Chief Executive, governor, general or captain.

Institution head.

Owner or editor of Newspapers or Magazines.

Owner or head of any business.

All 1's can buy or sell. If other vibrations emphasize their mental qualities, they are often found as writers and lawyers. If they incline to the creative side, many of the women are found as dressmakers and designers. They insist upon being left unhampered to carry out their own ideas.

NUMBER 2

Diplomat, statesman or politician.

Psychologist, student or teacher.

Secretary or office worker.

Statistician or compiler.

Detail worker.

Companion or Home-maker.

Artist (*chorus* singing or *group* dancing)

Psychic or medium.

All 2's are adapted to occupations where they work in association with others; they follow rather than lead. They are spokesmen for others and peace-makers for all. Because of their innate tact and desire for harmony, we find among them our greatest diplomats. Because of their instinctive response to the *rhythm* in all things we find among them fine musicians and dancers. They are most at home in the occupations where detail and minuteness are important.

NUMBER 3

Artist in words—Singer, writer, poet, dramatist, actor, speaker.

Artist in music—Singer, player—any instrument.

Artist on canvas, drawing, designing.

Critic—lecturing or writing.

Entertainer—stage, clubs or in society.

Society organizer or leader.

Welfare worker.

Clergyman or missionary.

Jeweller, milliner, decorator or dressmaker.

All 3's can sell because of their effective, imaginative methods of presentation. They are most at home in the cheerful and "decorative" occupations. The "mental" 3 takes naturally to writing; the emotional to acting and singing; the more frivolous to society and adornment.

NUMBER 4

Author of technical works.

Economist, technician, statistician.

Professor or instructor.

Organizer, executive, buyer.

Scientist. Accountant.

Skilled craftsman.

Physician or surgeon.

Chemist (manufacturing).

Electrician.

Builder, Master Mason, Contractor.
Horticulturist. Musician.

All 4's express best in material mediums. The highly mental choose to write or teach. They insist upon organization, system and accuracy. Among the women we find many seamstresses and many household drudges.

NUMBER 5

Senator, Civil Service Officer, Civic Leader.
Lawyer, Detective, Secret Service Chief.
Writer or editor.
Actor, Entertainer, Platform Speaker.
Promoter or "Barker."
Dramatic Critic, Theatrical Manager or Director.
Travelling salesman.
Professional courier.
Mining or electrical specialist.
Scientific inventor.

5's are "all things to all people." They make the best salesmen for they understand every angle of approach. They are "hail fellow well met" and welcomed in any crowd, so naturally succeed best at the occupations that bring them in contact with *people*. They are miserable if shut up in an office and must have perfect freedom of speech and action. They are born travellers.

NUMBER 6

Artist—Dramatic Actor or Musician.
Physician or Trained Nurse.
Hospital Chief, Welfare Worker, Institution Head of
    Personnel.
Teacher or Writer.
Hotel Executive, Restaurant or Tea-room Manager.
Dealer in food or home necessities.

Matron, Mother's Helper, Professional Guardian.
The "Cosmic" Father or Mother.

All 6's need a position of responsibility and trust. They regulate, harmonize and adjust. They are successful at all occupations connected with homes, institutions or projects to improve civil, educational or material conditions. They are concerned with the care of the old, the training of the young and the improvement of the entire community.

NUMBER 7

Law-maker, Judge, Lawyer.
Scientist, Mining or Electrical Expert.
Banker or Broker, Expert Accountant.
Expert Weaver or Watchmaker.
Inventor, Writer (Technical, Scientific or Philosophical), Editor.
University Dean or Administrator.
Clergyman—Priest, Bishop or Pope.
Naturalist, Horticulturist, Astronomer.
Occultist.
Authority on religions, ceremonials and church music.

7 gives us the "final word" in whatever form of expression he engages in—for he is a perfectionist and does not speak until he is *sure*. He is at home in any line of executive work which does not take him into the machinery-side of the business. He is the thinker and the sage.

NUMBER 8

Financier—Broker, Banker, Bondsman.
Director, Executive, Commercial Magnate.
Ship and Railroad Builder or Owner.
Manufacturer, Buyer or Seller on a large scale.
Corporation Head, Consultant, Promoter.
Newspaper Executive.

Expert on Commerce, Navigation, Transportation.

Art Patron (on the practical side).

Organizer of Charities.

"Big Business" is the slogan of the 8. He is most successful when concerned with the larger material issues of life. He always wins out if he keeps his breadth of outlook and admits no limitations.

NUMBER 9

Artist—in any line. (If actor, inclines to tragedy.)

Teacher, Healer, Preacher, Reformer.

Writer, Composer.

Art Patron (on the Art-side).

Judge, Criminal Lawyer, Advisor.

Doctor, Surgeon.

Philanthropist, Humanitarian.

9 gives freely of his emotions in all forms of Expression. He works best in those departments of life where inspiration, kindliness and human understanding are essential.

NUMBER 11

Evangelist, Minister, Reformer, Welfare Worker.

Psycho-analyst, Psychologist, Philosopher, Teacher.

Religious Writer, Charity Worker, Leader of Uplift Movements.

Actor (inspired), Explorer, Inventor.

All 11's seek to express their ideals. They are happiest when they can "turn on the light" of their own vision and inspiration. They are not adapted to the business world.

NUMBER 22

Builder, Shipper, Buyer in large concerns.

Teacher, Writer, Practical Reformer.

Leader, Ruler, Governor, Statesman.

Efficiency Expert.

Director of World Affairs.

Organizer of Public Works and Utilities.

Public Benefactor.

22 opens up new fields and builds the roads that make easy access to them. He establishes international communications and efficiently controls the whole—and all its parts. He beautifies while he builds.

What Do You Look Like?

Look at the people you know—including yourself—decide upon the "number" that fits the impression they make upon you, and then check up their Charts to see if it hasn't a prominent place *somewhere* in their make-up.

Your three principal numbers are your Soul Urge, your Expression and your Life Path. Do you *look* like any of them? Which?

Impression is a big factor in the world today. If you are doing what you want to do and have a contract for life, you don't have to worry about what you look like; but few are as secure as all that and many a big opportunity has been lost because we have failed to "look the part."

There is no infallible rule for *discovering* the Impression Number, for we make different impressions at different times, but you will do well to carefully consult the "Table of the Impression," relate the numbers to your own Soul Urge, Expression and Life Path and then strive to look and act the "number" that will help you the most.

We have remarked that the *usual Im*pression is that

of the *Ex*pression. We do not wear our hearts upon our sleeves, so our outward appearance cannot inform the world as to our Soul Number; people must *know* us in order to label us correctly. That eliminates our vowels. No one ever sees our Quiescent Self, so that eliminates the consonants. What of the total?

We usually take on a certain amount of color from the job we are continually engaged in. If we are a Big Executive, we usually wear an air of efficiency and general prosperity; if we are the mother of a large family we either look comfortable and satisfied (positive) or worried and anxious (negative); if we are obliged to drudge all day at tiresome detail, we usually look lined and discouraged. We are all in danger of growing to *look* like what we *do*. If we want to (and it is sometimes a good thing) well and good; we can encourage ourselves in it: if we don't want to, we can change it. Look at the Table and choose wisely.

TABLE OF THE IMPRESSION

NUMBER 1

Original, Forceful, Dominant. Strong physique. Wear heavy stripes or patterns; decided colors.
If negative—No distinction; a drab personality.

NUMBER 2

Sweet and subdued; Soft-voiced, Retiring, Shy. Usually plump. Wear neutral shades; never gaudy.
If negative—Slack (often dirty), Run-down heels; Self-conscious.

NUMBER 3

Attractive, Bristling with Personality. Animated and Talkative. Always well dressed, in perfect color combinations. The women like shirrings, ruffles and lace. 3 sets the fashion.
If negative—Round-shouldered, Awkward, Showy, Inharmonious.

NUMBER 4

Solid, Precise, Dignified, Tailor-made. Tall, sometimes bony. Wear excellent and durable materials; plain colors.
If negative—Lined faces, thin lips, severe angles, proud of their plainness.

NUMBER 5

Striking, Attracting attention. Entertaining. Faulty physique. Wear daring colors and unusual combinations.
If negative—Loud, bizarre, loaded with cheap jewelry, heavy make-up.

NUMBER 6

Quiet, harmonious, good taste. Comfortable-looking. Fatherly or motherly. Wear good clothes and good colors, but prefer comfort to style. Create an atmosphere of harmony and well-being.
If negative—Slouchy, fat, ungroomed, careless, inefficient.

NUMBER 7

Quiet, aloof, poised, refined, unruffled. Slim hands and feet. Always beautifully and harmoniously dressed. The women wear pastel shades.

If negative—Nervous, chattering, attracting attention to hide embarrassment. Vulgar. Wear coarse materials and bad color combinations.

NUMBER 8

Prosperous, attractive, radiating strength and efficiency. Strong physique, dominant personality. Inclined to pomp and display. Genial, sociable. Wear heavy, expensive-looking materials. Careful of details (spats, gloves, shoes, neckties); fastidious.
If negative—Sullen, mean, over-worked. Wear cheap, unpressed clothing. Careless of detail; loud-voiced.

NUMBER 9

Romantic, artistic, beautiful, strong, virile, youthful. Impressive personality. Courteous, kindly, impulsive, emotional. Always well-dressed and well-groomed. Beauty and harmony in material and colors.
If negative—Over-anxious to please; striving for impressions; craving attention; full of empty promises. Wear clothes for effect. Careless in grooming.

NUMBER 11

Refined, spiritual, "inspired"-looking, with a far-away light in their eyes. Vibrant personality.
Wear beautiful, smooth materials of the finest texture.
If negative—Love pomp and ceremony; insist upon running everything. Wear coarse clothes and loud colors.

NUMBER 22

Harmony and power combined. Want much space and air. Nervous and energetic, but poised and capable-look-

ing. Tactful, congenial, kind. Wear clothes that are no-
ticeable for their correctness and good coloring.

If negative—No power. Hard, discontented faces. Repressed, or cold and bullying. Clothes loud, unattractive,
sloppy.

CHAPTER IV

FOLLOWING YOUR LIFE PATH

This Is Your Destiny

Your Life Path is found from your birthdate—the sum of the month, day and year you were born.

It is your Initiation into what you came to do and to become—your Destiny!

We always reduce to a single number in Numerology, for we want to know the *Essence* of the different vibrations that make the final result. This rule holds in figuring the Life Path from the birthdate (with the exception of the Master Numbers, 11 and 22).

Months are numbered according to their position in the calendar.

January, the *first* month, is 1; February, the *second* month, is 2, etc. down to October, the 10th month, which is 1, November, the 11th month, which is 11 (a Master number) and December, the 12th month, which is 3.

Days are numbered according to their calendar number and are likewise reduced (except the 11th and 22nd).

Years are numbered according to their digits on the calendar—as $1931=1+9+3+1=14,=5$. They are reduced unless their total is 11 or 22.

$1901=1+9+0+1=11$ (unreduced).
$1876=1+8+7+6=22$ (unreduced).

To Find the Life Path

For example:—George Washington was born February 22nd, 1732

February   22nd   1732

2   +22   + 4   =28, =1 Life Path
of George Washington

Herbert Hoover was born August 10th, 1874.

August   10th   1874.

8   +1   + 2   =11 Life Path
of Herbert Hoover

In the first example, the 22 of George Washington's birthdate is one of the parts or "Cycles" of his Life Path and we do not *see* it in the total. We must remember, however, that there is a "22" behind the final digit and it must not be lost sight of by reducing it to 4.

In the second example, the final sum of 11 must not be thought of as 2.

The number of the *day* on which you were born is a highly important factor in your life. These numbers will be treated in a separate Table.

TABLE OF THE LIFE PATH

1. INDIVIDUALIZATION

Must learn independence and have the ability to "go it alone."

Must strengthen your own powers, use your brain to devise new and original methods, and *create*. Must refuse limitations, cooperate without losing the individuality, lead, control and direct. Must develop the body, mind and spirit to the highest point of efficiency.

You will find your opportunity by making yourself invaluable in any position in which you find yourself and will thus gain quick promotion to leadership. The appeal on the 1-Path is to individuals rather than to crowds. Its element is FIRE. It is most at home in the North.

2. Association

Must learn to submerge yourself and follow the lead of others. Must be the peacemaker, diplomat and go-between. Must work carefully and patiently on the smallest detail, governed by the idea of service and cooperation. Must learn the power of silence. Must be a good mixer. Must not look for personal praise or recognition. Must consider as important kindness, gentleness and the feelings of others. Must cultivate friendships and be loyal to them. Must put yourself under the law of giving and receiving. Must be expressive only through patience and persistence—never dominantly. Must listen and absorb.

You will find your opportunity in diplomacy and among your many friends, who will do your fighting for you. The appeal on the 2-Path is to groups or communities. Its element is WATER. It is adaptable anywhere, but happiest near the sea.

3. Self-expression

Must learn to give of yourself—freely and joyously. Must cultivate social contacts and be always a welcome addition to any gathering. Must make yourself invaluable through your ability to shed the light on dark places. Must learn to express yourself through art and beauty, friends and happiness.

You will find your opportunity on the lighter side of life, mingling in society and doing the pleasant things. You should seek the type of occupation that gives you a chance to express artistically. You must seize every occasion to use WORDS—whether in speaking, acting, singing or writing. The appeal on the 3-Path is to both individuals and crowds. Its element is FIRE. (See 1.)

4. ORGANIZATION

Must learn strict attention to duty. This initiation seldom includes travel or expansion. You must learn to serve and produce. Must rise above any seeming limitation and make perfect and substantial the form of the thing at hand.

You will find your opportunity deep, if not varied. You will have a chance to build for lasting benefit and to teach others less evolved than yourself. This Path holds possibilities of *great* attainment. Patience, service and dependability will bring the rewards. The appeal on the 4-Path is to communities. Its element is EARTH. It works wherever it is sent and is apt to *stick*.

5. FREEDOM

Must expect frequent change, variety, travel and the unexpected. Must learn the right use of freedom. Must learn foreign languages and understand all classes and conditions of people. Must be alert to seize all that is novel and progressive. Must adapt yourself to unusual circumstances and conditions. Must exercise ingenuity and follow various angles of development. Must constantly seek the new and untried—profiting by every experience.

You will find your opportunity away from the beaten track, if you will learn the lesson of *discard* and not remain in a rut. You will meet scientific, inventive and resourceful people who will benefit you, if you make the effort to find them. You will grow by adapting yourself to change and uncertainty. The appeal on the 5-Path is to crowds and audiences. Its element is AIR. It works only when it is *free*, whether in the desert, on mountain heights or when travelling.

6. ADJUSTMENT

Must learn the meaning of responsibility. Must be able to adjust inharmonious conditions and situations, in your own life and in the lives of those with whom you come in contact. Must serve cheerfully, efficiently and quietly, learning how to balance opposites. Must meet the problems of domesticity and assume many burdens belonging to the weaker brethren for whom you are responsible. Must be ready to give material or spiritual aid whenever called upon. Must maintain your own ideals at all times, but never seek to "adjust" by forcing them on others. Must be ready to serve the family, the community or the universe—if necessary.

You will find your opportunity in the valuable service you will render to those in need of spiritual or material adjustment. The appeal on the 6-Path is to the family, community, state or world. It is governed by two elements—EARTH and AIR—material welfare or transmuted (impersonal) love.

7. Wisdom. Aloneness

Must learn the power of keen mental analysis. Must seek wisdom and the hidden truths. Must develop subjectively, in order to be a fit priest and counsellor. Must learn to be alone and not lonely. Must work on theories and fundamentals. Must continually increase your store of useful knowledge. Must not concern yourself with the accumulation of material possessions and must learn that he who loses his life (materially) shall find it (spiritually). You must apply spiritual laws to material affairs. Must rest, study, meditate, worship, be *silent* and know yourself. Must not insist upon partnerships or leadership. Must learn to understand the unseen world.

You will find your opportunity through what is *brought* to you rather than through what you seek for yourself; in quiet places, away from bustle and confusion. The appeal on the 7-Path is to individuals who need life theories. Its element is WATER—deep and still.

8. POWER. MATERIAL FREEDOM

Must be in the world of commercial activity, business affairs, power and achievement. Must cultivate a large outlook and refuse all limitation. Must develop efficiency and management. Must learn how to oil and *run* the machinery. Must deal with the uninspirational, practical and material things of life and eschew dreams, visions and impracticalities. Must understand the laws that govern money—its accumulation, its power and its use.

You will find your opportunity among people and conditions of wealth and those in need of efficiency and executive ability. The appeal on the 8-Path is to large corporations or organizations. Its element is EARTH.

9. UNIVERSALITY. THE BROTHERHOOD OF MAN

Must learn to be the complete humanitarian and welfare worker. Must learn to love and serve your fellow man. Must abandon all prejudices of race or caste, realizing the basic universality of all peoples. Must place all others before yourself. Must expect to be used and to give up all personal ambitions and possessions if the general good demands it. You must attract all things but hold to nothing. You must settle down nowhere, but consider the world your fireside. You must learn the Law of Fulfilment, for this is the end of a series of initiations. You must give your love, sympathy, help and understanding without stint.

You will find your opportunity among emotional, artistic and inspirational people—for you are to learn of the highest vibration of the artist. The appeal on the 9-Path is to the Many or the ALL. Its element is FIRE.

11. REVELATION

Must specialize in subjectivity. Must elevate everything to the plane of inspiration. Must be the ultra-specialist—developing talents of invention or seeking the discovery of new principles. Must investigate mysticism and put it to its highest use. Must trust your intuitions and have faith in a higher guidance. Must be ever on the alert to learn the type of illumination and revelation that you are to give to the world. You should never strive for accumulation (the 2) and avoid any tendency toward *hoarding*—realizing that 11 is to *shed* a light of his own. You should inspire by your own example, *living* the Truth that is revealed to you. You should live humbly in the limelight.

You will find your opportunity in the preaching of the gospel—be it along spiritual lines or in the realms of invention or acting. You are liable to achieve great fame if you do not seek it from ulterior motives. The appeal on the 11-Path is to the inspirational, artistic idealists, and to those in need of spiritual uplift. Its element is AIR.

22. MATERIAL MASTER.

Must learn service on a large and constructive scale. Must use your power from a spiritual and idealistic angle. You must make magnificent and uplifting the useful and practical. You must base construction and organization upon social principles.

You will find your opportunity in international movements or great commercial, philanthropic and political institutions, affairs of government, rulership of countries, etc. You will have the chance to make the dream of Peace, Love, Happiness, Work and Prosperity come true. The appeal on the 22-Path is to masses, governments, countries and races that are in need of improvement and expansion. Its element is WATER.

TABLE OF THE BIRTHDAYS

The vibration of the day on which you were born (found from its number on the calendar) has a great deal of influence on your Life Path and is of much assistance in helping you to choose the right vocation. Its effect is carried with you all through life, but it is most active between your 28th and 56th years.

It is one of the three divisions or "Cycles" *behind* your Life Path number, but is the most important, in many ways, as it concerns the whole middle or "flowering" period of your life.

Consult this Table and learn how you may expect to develop as you follow the Path set for you.*

If your birthday falls on the ——

FIRST DAY OF THE MONTH

You have a strong will, are self-reliant and independent. You like to plan but not to build. You are inclined to procrastinate. You can diagnose better than prescribe. You have a good mind, like to reason things out and refer most things to your head rather than your heart. You are practical and idealistic at the same time. You are capable of great devotion but are not usually demonstrative. You like to be encouraged, and with all your independence, are very sensitive. You have a great deal of unexpressed power.

* All students of Numerology are indebted to Mrs. Cochran for much material and illumination on the subject of birthdates, from a Western viewpoint.

Second Day of the Month

You are very emotional and keenly sensitive to the atmosphere in which you find yourself. You are a little nervous and absent-minded, but you make friends easily and are much loved by them. You like to have people make a fuss over you for you are very warm-hearted yourself and crave affection. You should avoid moods and all things that have a tendency to depress you. You like material ease and comfort, even though you are not always inclined to make an effort to get it. You should write poetry or in some other way cultivate your talent for rhythm and music.

Third Day of the Month

You have a great deal of vitality and quickly "come back" from any illness. Your imagination is vivid and you can make a good story out of the most insignificant incident. You should write or engage in some line of work that would give your critical and literary ability a chance to shine. You should have a variety of interests and keep yourself very busy. You are intense and extreme in affection, have great emotional crises, but are quickly restored. You love society and many people, are very expressive in public and at your best when you have an audience. You are easily satisfied and make the best of conditions. You are restless and should have some interest outside of home or work to keep you occupied.

Fourth Day of the Month

You are a great lover of nature, your home, your family and your country. You would succeed very well in a

manufacturing business, building, utilities or textiles—
also in any occupation connected with the products of
the earth. You should engage in music, painting or sculpture as a side-line, although you could commercialize any
of these. You are rather set in your views and inclined to
impose them on others—feeling yourself to be master of
the correct code of ethics. You suffer a great deal through
your love nature, for your belief in discipline makes it
difficult for you to express all the love you feel or get
all you want. You are a tireless worker and inclined to
drive others. You should insist upon cheerfulness and
take time off to play—otherwise you are likely to spend
your savings in paying doctors' bills.

Fifth Day of the Month

You are very adaptable, a good booster and something
of a boaster. You are very imaginative and love embel-
lishments and trimmings. You have a fine mind and are
very versatile. You are excellent company and usually
keep things moving rapidly. You love life, all sorts of
experiences—changing from one thing to another with
great rapidity. You would do well in chemistry, mining,
law or the brokerage business. You should be married,
but you would refuse to be tied down by home—or anything else. You have a good voice and could give much
pleasure with your singing.

Sixth Day of the Month

Love is the keynote of your nature. You long for praise
and appreciation and are made thoroughly unhappy by
criticism. You want companionship and lavish your af-

fection upon one "nearest and dearest"—for the duration of the attachment, but, since the 6 is always searching for its ideal and seldom finds it, you like to try again and again, so are apt to earn for yourself the reputation of fickleness. You love children but children of your own are not necessary to your happiness. You are well protected, but are in constant dread of the poorhouse. You are mental without being intellectual. You have fine powers of imitation and could succeed on the stage if your Life Path presented the opportunity; you could also do well in business and would find it an easy matter to acquire money or backing for your enterprises. You have literary and artistic tendencies and are not attracted to mechanics. You must have people around you and congenial surroundings.

Seventh Day of the Month

You should learn to specialize. You have a keen brain and are capable of deep mental analysis. You should never gamble or speculate and should examine thoroughly every detail of any enterprise in which you are engaged. You should never take advice against your own intuitions—which are very strong. You must WAIT and not seek. You have talent for stringed instruments or the organ. You have excellent judgment in money matters and would succeed as a banker or a broker (especially if you have a prominent 8 in your name or on your Path). You have decided opinions and dislike to change them. You should avoid marriage in this Cycle, for it is not easy to make physical adjustments in the 7. Whenever possible, take time off to go to the country and rest, meditate and relax. Spend a portion of each day *alone*.

EIGHTH DAY OF THE MONTH

You are creative and productive and should choose a business career which is progressive and expansive and which deals with matters of general or public interest. You must not enter into equal partnerships, but be at the head of your own business. You could engage successfully in the banking business, be a railroad president, the head of a large corporation or organization or an efficient public servant. You must always express honesty and integrity for permanent success. You are more fond of books than you are of reading. You are inclined to large gestures, giving great sums of money to institutions or becoming a collector or benefactor of art. You are fond of display and like to have your family a credit to you.

NINTH DAY OF THE MONTH

You are in the vibration of publicity, distribution, art, broadmindedness and philanthropy. You are inclined to metaphysics and like to relate them to world problems. You are literary and artistic, have a strong will and are a natural ruler. You can succeed in practically any artistic line and may be attracted to writing, teaching, the law, the ministry or publishing. You should have a broad education and be allowed to choose your own profession. You are emotional and strong-willed. You belong in the world and *to* it and can rarely lead a purely personal life with success. Avoid marriage in this Cycle, as 9 is a "finisher" and there is apt to be a break-up of the relationship—either through death or some other form of separation—although the love may remain intact. You will take long journeys and be subject to many changes.

TENTH DAY OF THE MONTH

You should have many interests, as you are capable of efficiently handling a variety of things at the same time. You are apt to feel somewhat isolated and bereft, for many depend upon you but few help you. You have a fine mind and a strong will. You are jealous of your own friends and possessions—and very exclusive in these directions. You are an excellent promoter of those enterprises in which you have faith. You have much creative talent and, although you belong in the business world, should cultivate art as a side-line—preferably music or painting. You are very hospitable but not very domestic and should not be overburdened with the affairs of the home. You have much vitality and easily recover from physical or emotional ills.

ELEVENTH DAY OF THE MONTH

You have much determination and perseverance but your energies and desires are apt to be fluctuating. You are very dramatic in thought and action, brilliant and scintillating, but nervous and high-strung within. You have swift reactions and must be careful that your intellect does not submerge your intuitions. You are apt to impose your own code of morals too rigidly and not make sufficient allowance for the human equation. Your loves and emotions are extreme and without reason. You must guard your health and nerves and continually fight against overbalance. You must avoid any inclination to be mercenary or to accumulate money for your own pedestal. You are subject to extremes—on the heights or in the depths. Remember that you are given a Master Number.

TWELFTH DAY OF THE MONTH

You are brilliant, magnetic and imaginative, very convincing in an argument and an excellent speaker. You are fond of life and action and have a well-balanced mind. You would make an excellent trial lawyer, promoter or actor. You have high ideals and many artistic tendencies and you should train yourself for a "mission" in life. You must be kept intellectually active in order to avoid the tendency to "ups and downs" which is the handicap of all 3's. You have a great flair for design and would make a fine architect. You are somewhat inclined to flirtations and affairs. Finish what you begin and avoid the tendency to scatter.

THIRTEENTH DAY OF THE MONTH

This is a number of contradiction and some difficulty—creation, expansion and restlessness behind the law of regularity and limitation ($1+3=4$). You are sensitive and spiritual, suffer through your environment and are subject to fits of explosion. You have a good mind but a very set and stubborn will. You have a strong love nature but seldom show it and always suffer because of it. You are frequently misunderstood and considered temperamental and, at times, unreasonable. You are inclined to be dictatorial, but are an excellent manager. You can design, woodcarve or "sculp"—as a side-line but would succeed best in a mercantile or real estate business—building, buying or selling. Your best success is in dealing with the earth—mining, geology and practical construction. You love a uniform but hate war. Home is vital to your happiness.

FOURTEENTH DAY OF THE MONTH

You are versatile—and dual, having both a reasoning and prophetic mind. You are very "lucky" in taking chances and are a natural bettor and gambler. You are not inherently artistic but need some form of art-expression for recreation. You should go into business on a large scale and manage your own affairs. You should marry very young, for you are apt to crave frequent changes in later life. You are very emotional and can always be appealed to through your feelings and sympathies. You should avoid all the pitfalls lying in wait for the physical body—drink, sex and the senses. You are a bridge between the physical and the spiritual worlds and have great constructive or destructive power.

FIFTEENTH DAY OF THE MONTH

You are under the protection of the kindly, harmonious 6. You have many gifts and should achieve much financial success. You *absorb* knowledge rather than acquire it by hard study. You attract to yourself many things—friends, gifts and opportunities. You are capable of much self-sacrifice and will serve a just cause or a loved friend unselfishly, but you will not submit to domination. You are inclined to a professional career and as a lawyer, doctor, diplomat or statesman would do your best work. Your mind is scientific (through the 1 and the 5) but your expression is often musical (through the 6). You always give the impression of youthfulness and, if you remain active, of abounding health. You are generous and demonstrative and more inciined to personal charities than to general philanthropy. You love your home.

Sixteenth Day of the Month

You are inclined to nervousness and are sometimes considered irritable. You are apt to make complications and intricacies for yourself and suffer through the consequences. You are inclined to the natural aloofness of the 7, but lean toward home and affection through the 6. If you choose art or literature as your profession you should have some business interest on the outside to which you could apply your fine powers of reason and analysis. You do not like to have your plans interfered with, although you are not actively aggressive. You are inclined to procrastination and live too much within yourself. You want affection but do not always make the effort to *earn* it.

Seventeenth Day of the Month

You are high-minded and proud-spirited, conservative by fits and starts, generous or penurious, collecting or scattering. You are very set in your ideas and seldom yield to others. You are in one of the best banking and financial vibrations there is—$(1+7=8)$, and can conserve and manage the interests and affairs of others with great success. You should be the actual head of your own business, but should work with under-partners or associates. You *execute* what you undertake and should deal in large affairs—taking care, however, that there is some one to attend to the details—for you hate to be concerned with them. The final digit of this number rules the earth and you will do well in any enterprise connected with it— such as lands, mines, oil or live stock. You have great love of knowledge and are fond of exploring. Any writing you do will incline to the technical and historical rather than to fiction. You want *proof* in spiritual matters.

EIGHTEENTH DAY OF THE MONTH

You will have much change, activity and travel. Great things will be expected of you, for you are given the independent 1 and the efficient 8 to broadcast through the 9, so you may find yourself burdened with the care of the old or helpless or with groups or communities who will tap your fund of helpfulness. You do not like to take advice, and are seldom in need of it. You may find yourself inclined to law, politics or religion—any *large* field that needs efficient administration. Your first efforts may not always be successful, but you will succeed on repetition. While somewhat emotional (through the 9) you are strongly intellectual and fond of reasoning and arguing. You would make an excellent dramatic critic or writer— also a good orator. You are never rash in money matters, feeling the responsibility *behind* your 9. Marriages or engagements in this Cycle are apt to be annulled or broken.

NINETEENTH DAY OF THE MONTH

This vibration runs the whole gamut of the numbers from 1....9. You are logical, persevering, tenacious, practical, artistic and universal. You must be independent and not submit to limitations. You can rise to great heights or fall to great depths, both in acts and emotions. You do not like conventions or subscribe to them in your private life, but will never give offense in public. You are very versatile and can succeed at a number of things—notably law, music or as a medical specialist.

You belong to the professions rather than the business lines of activity. You would make an excellent political worker—if allowed your head—for you have a deep sense of responsibility. You will be called upon to make many adjustments in your personal life. You have a deep aversion to inferiority and a strong impulse to better conditions. You crave change and variety and are always making alterations in your surroundings.

TWENTIETH DAY OF THE MONTH

You will find your best milieu in a small business and in an atmosphere of friendliness and protection. You are rather disinclined to branch out into the larger fields of affairs and are content to work with others rather than assume too much responsibility on your own. You would be an excellent politician or clergyman—although you talk better on paper than before crowds. You are sympathetic and affectionate. You are capable of accumulating a store of knowledge and should have a good education. You would do well in corporation law or the management of estates—where attention to detail is an important factor. You have a strong affinity for the country and for your own home, family and friends. You want to help but are rather averse to manual labor. You should express musically—not as soloist, but in the chorus or orchestra.

TWENTY-FIRST DAY OF THE MONTH

You have a beautiful voice, and while you may have difficulties to encounter in training it for public singing, its speaking qualities are sure to give pleasure and prove an asset. You are magnetic and musical, fond of beauty, art and dancing. You are highly nervous and should work to control some of your unaccountable aversions to things and people. You are more receptive than active in your expressions of love, but you take great pride and interest in the objects of your affections. You are a better friend than marriage companion, for you are inclined to suspicions through your imaginative qualities. You must avoid any tendency to brood or become morbid. Your 3 will lead your interests to books, publishing, papers and editorship. You will be very successful in any educational line.

TWENTY-SECOND DAY OF THE MONTH

Again a Master Number! You will function in the objective and subjective world and must be ever on your guard to keep your balance between the two. Like all high-powered numbers, 22 is nervous and over-stimulated and in need of much rest and seclusion to find and keep his equilibrium. You are very intuitional and should rely on your first impressions. You are constantly pulled between the expression of your ideals and the desire to keep them within conservative and constructive limits. You have unlimited *power* on both planes, but you have also the high mission to fulfill of *universal* utilitarianism and cannot afford to have many personal ambitions. You would make an excellent corporation lawyer, mining engineer, assayer, geologist or conserver of public interests. You can deal in vast tracts of real estate, but should not try to be a landlord yourself. Avoid any doubtful business transactions—gambling, bootlegging, etc.—you would be sure to be caught at it and suffer in consequence. Your greatest success is in the world of *form* where you have supreme control. You can succeed in any line that meets with your ideals. There are many great poets, inventors and musicians in the 22—and those who have achieved name and fame for *themselves* have made some contribution to the *general* good—the requirement of the 22!

TWENTY-THIRD DAY OF THE MONTH

You are very sympathetic, sensitive and understanding. You have a practical turn of mind that makes you very valuable to many classes of people. Your digit of 5 (the physical body) gives you an uncanny ability to diagnose all physical ailments and you would make a great success as a nurse or doctor—in general practice but not surgery—as the mission of this number is to build and heal rather than tear down and destroy. Your technical and practical ability would also give you an interest in chemistry, the law or the brokerage business. You are too practical to succeed in art. You are not burdened with any inferiority complex and are thoroughly self-sufficient. You are popular and fond of social contacts. You make the best of any situation and get much out of life. You are willing to assume many burdens and are a fine companion.

TWENTY-FOURTH DAY OF THE MONTH

With this birthdate you must keep very active or you will suffer from wasted energies. You will concentrate on one thing at a time but you will crave frequent change. You must not plan to *retire* from business, but keep on expanding and enlarging. You are strongly *allied* to art, music and sculpture, have considerable talent for the stage and are thoroughly dramatic in nature, but you will have financial success as a banker, promoter or merchant; you can also make money in real estate. You are practical, but a little inclined to dream. Externals count for little with you and you have not much appreciation of the value of time or money. You have a decided domestic quality and a highly developed ego. You are inclined to magnify your joys and sorrows. Avoid depression, jealousy and worry. You will learn much through your powers of observation.

TWENTY-FIFTH DAY OF THE MONTH

You are naturally prophetic and intuitive and have a strong leaning toward occultism. You are not always understood for you have a tendency to conceal your real feelings and emotions. You have a talent for painting, sculpture and wood-carving and can commercialize almost any department of art to which you incline. You have a fine voice and can sing and play. You could also succeed along professional lines or in business and should work into politics and interest yourself in its more constructive side. You are inclined to be vacillating, and if you do not overcome this tendency, your affairs are likely to suffer from this malady. You need to learn concentration and force your mind into stability and away from erraticism, self-depreciation and melancholy. Your weakness lies in your affections. You must always keep to the "steep and narrow way" for there is a great tendency in this number to wander from the path of rectitude. Those of this birth are apt to preach morals but practice over-freedom. You are idealistic and hopeful. Work against laziness.

TWENTY-SIXTH DAY OF THE MONTH

Nothing is too small for practical use. You are very introspective and given to live in the past—to the detriment of the present or the future. You start many things but find it difficult to see them through. You should choose a profession in one of the artistic lines—but not in music. This you could commercialize in a large way. You rise superior to conditions or fall below the average—as you choose. You should have a good education. If your taste does not incline you to art, you would make a success of politics, diplomacy or as a social secretary. You have a beautiful domestic nature, love home and children and should marry early. You are fastidious about your personal belongings and are fond of show and color in dress. You do not insist upon physical comforts and are very generous to others.

TWENTY-SEVENTH DAY OF THE MONTH

This is one of the "4th dimensional" numbers and is rather more materially inclined than the other 9's. It is a strong marriage vibration, but, as has been said before, marriage in a 9 Cycle is apt to be disappointing. There is a tendency to wander for the numbers beyond 26 (the letters of the alphabet) have no dwelling place of their own and must "borrow the temple". You are forceful, quietly determined and somewhat erratic. You are a natural leader and cannot be in a subordinate position. You would be a good lawyer and a great diplomat, a successful broker or stock-dealer. You do not like to account for your conduct, are ardent in your affections and are apt to overdo family traits. You are versatile

and artistic and through the 2 are a very clever sculptor.
You have literary talents and religious tendencies and
your trend of belief is toward the wisdom of the East and
away from orthodoxy. You could be a journalist, author,
lecturer or teacher, for you have all the necessary qualities for literary attainment.

TWENTY-EIGHTH DAY OF THE MONTH

This is the most affectionate of all the 1's. You are
strong-willed, dominant and tenacious, but full of affection and willing to break all the traditions in the calendar
for its sake. Your unions are apt to be unconventional,
but will always represent your ideals. You are executive
by nature and would be successful as an architect or
engineer, teacher, lecturer or lawyer. You want to excel
and will make great sacrifices to further your ambitions.
You must avoid any tendency to laziness, for you will
soon acquire a habit of day-dreaming and trifling that
will nullify your splendid gifts. You are inclined to magnify everything that concerns your own life and thus
subject yourself to many disappointments. You love freedom and suffer from restraint and limitation. When your
ideals are realized you usually drop them, causing your
final success to fade into oblivion.

TWENTY-NINTH DAY OF THE MONTH

You are spiritual and inspired ($2+9=11$) and capable
of leadership to great results. You can adjust labor problems and unify religious differences. Through your great
power you can bring to yourself and others great honor
or destruction. You are an extremist in all things—intense in love and judgments, depressed or joyful. You

have nerves that must be watched and governed lest they run away with you. Home is necessary for your happiness but you are not always easy to live with for you are absorbed in your own dreams and affairs and forget to consider the comfort of others. You have many moods and should have a definite work to keep you poised and efficient.

THIRTIETH DAY OF THE MONTH

You are filled with electricity and vitality, are rather nervous, but do not attract diseases and ailments, and if they come to you, have great power to throw them off. You must guard against all obsessions and never indulge in idle excursions into the astral realms. You are set in your opinions and apt to think you are invariably right in your conclusions. You have a little knowledge (and must seek more) and much imagination and intuition. You are a fine companion and would make an excellent teacher, writer or social worker. You are fundamentally loyal, although you are inclined to be flirtatious. You like appreciation for your good deeds. You are an excellent manager, but are not over-fond of work.

THIRTY-FIRST DAY OF THE MONTH

Like the 30th birthdate, you should never *play* with psychic phenomena. Your aspirations are not always within reason and are likely to bring you disappointments. You must cultivate the force and application that belong to the 4 if you would make a success of your life. You have good business qualities but would find decoration or writing a more congenial line of work. You would be an excellent chemist or alchemist for you have great originality in the combining of drugs and medicines. You love travel and do not like to live alone. You should marry early for responsibility is necessary for your stabilization. You never forget a kindness—nor an injury. You must learn the law and power of finances for you have a tendency to scatter them improvidently.

SUMMARY OF THE ESSENTIALS

Example Charts

(1) SOUL URGE; Quiescent Self; (2) EXPRES
SION; (3) LIFE PATH; Birthday.

```
      6       +      10 – 1      +        14 – 5      = 12 = 3 Soul Urge
     1    5     1 3   3    3      9        5
   C H A R L E S   A U G U S T U S   L I N D B E R G H
   3 8   9 3   1       7    1 2    1    3   5    2   9 7 8
      24 – 6              11              38 – 11     = 28 = 1 Quiescent Self
   3 8 1 9 3 5 1     1 3 7 3 1 2 3 1     3 9 5 4 2 5 9 7 8
      30 – 3     +      21 – 3     +        52 – 7     = 13 = 4 Expression
```

```
               February 4th   1902
                  2  + 4  +  3  . . . . . . . . . . . . . . . . . 9 Life Path
                          4th . . . . . . . . . . . . . . 4 Birthday
```

```
      10 – 1      +      17 – 8      +     7      = 16 = 7 Soul Urge
     9     1      5    5    7         7
   R I C H A R D    E V E L Y N    B Y R D
   9   3 8    9 4    4    3    5    2    9 4
      33 – 6      +      12 – 3      +   15 – 6    = 15 = 6 Quiescent Self
   9 9 3 8 1 9 4    5 4 5 3 7 5    2 7 9 4
      43 – 7      +      29 – 11     +    22      = 40 = 4 Expression
```

```
            October   25th   1888
               1  + 7  +  7          = 15 = 6 Life Path
                         7th =       7 Birthday
```

YOUR OWN CHART

Set up your own Chart on this page, following the form in the examples given.

CHAPTER V

SHOULD YOU CHANGE YOUR NAME?

YES and NO. If you thoroughly dislike it; if you think you have outgrown it; if it makes you unhappy or dissatisfied; if it seems a hopeless misfit with what you want to do and can do; if you are consistently unsuccessful—YES.

If you think to escape your Destiny; if you expect to be relieved of your responsibilities; if you count on having it remove all thorns from a promised bed of roses, or transform the harvest of former plantings—NO.

We are placed, chorded, colored, numbered and *named* before we arrive on this scene of action and we cannot *select* our own vibrations, for each one is a part of the ineradicable *label* placed upon us by the Creator of all things.

We all have certain adjustments to make, certain lessons to learn and a certain Destiny to fulfill—and sometimes the job is too much for us. In the last analysis we escape *nothing*, but there are certain periods of the life when the accumulation of adjustments crowds too thickly upon us and we need help to extricate ourselves from the network. Or it may be that our Path of Opportunity gives us the Big Chance that our name-vibration cannot live up to. Or we may have satisfied the original requirements of our Expression and "outgrown" it—and are ready for a new angle of development. Or our own name may have fallen into disrepute because of some "wild oats" member of the family. OR—and this is the rarest case of all—we *may* have been incorrectly named in the first place.

"My parents gave me the wrong name!"

This is the usual cry of the person who wants to change his name—and nine times out of ten he is wrong.

The Soul has taken many journeys in the past and *knows* its present needs. The Soul wants progress upward on the Great Spiral and *chooses* for the incarnating ego the Vowels whose total shall accomplish this purpose. This is the Urge you bring with you. This, together with the other letters of your name, sums up your past experiences and allows you to Express the things you are most familiar with.

There is a strong covenant between the child and the parents; there is a long "Dark Cycle" before the child is born, and during this Dark Cycle the vibrations that are to label the new life are so impressed upon the subconscious minds of the parents that they are impelled to carry out the plan. If, however, there is confusion in their minds, disagreement and dissension, interference on the part of relatives and a final grudging compromise, the child may come into life with a misfit name that not only increases his difficulties, but often seriously affects his health. When he is old enough to think for himself he will drop it and give himself another, or his friends will do it for him. He and his own vibrations will find each other.

Many instances have been known of names decided upon by parents—after much controversy—and at the moment of baptism or record, an entirely different one pronounced; which only goes to prove that the subconscious mind is working regardless of the one we are most familiar with.

Many instances also have been known of babies named before birth choosing their own birthdates—for "easier going" in later life. In these cases, unless the doctor and the mother are Numerologists, they wonder at the premature or delayed arrival, as the case may be.

Be assured that, in all probability, you were correctly named in the beginning and that now, if you want to make a change, for some reason other than from passing whim or fancy, there is probably a good reason for it and the new name will doubtless work out to your temporary, if not lasting, benefit.

Be careful, however, if you are thinking of doing the job yourself, that you thoroughly understand every phase and angle of your present vibrations and that you know how to relate the new ones to those that are fixed and unalterable. Every uttered sound sets up a vibration of harmony or discord, with results that are beneficial or disastrous. If you are not thoroughly proficient in the Science of Number, consult the best Numerologist you can find to help you.

While we never escape the urge of the soul, the Destiny determined by the Life Path or the "lacks" we have to make up, we may gain many advantages by attracting to ourselves *external* aids that will promote our success and speed up our opportunities.

There are many examples in the Bible of names changed for definite and specific reasons. The Lord changed the names of Sara and Abram to SaraH and AbraHam when

He promised them a son (H is a child-bearing letter).

Simon, already a successful business man, was to be made head of the church, the Lord said to him, "Thou art Peter (P-7) and upon this rock will I build my Church".

Today, in Java, when a member of a family is on his death-bed, his distracted friends and relatives often give him a new name, thinking to ward off death. If they succeed in so short a time, there are doubtless other contributing causes—but their faith is a tribute to Number.

Nicknames and pet names show how you stand with the people who give them to you.* The Williams and Richards and Henrys usually mean something different to every member of the family.

Points to be Considered in Changing the Name

We must always look first at the Life Path, for that indicates the only type of opportunity we are given; it would be folly to select deliberately a set of vibrations that could find no outlet for their expression.

We must next consider our abilities—even before our desires—for it is safer to use the tools with which we are familiar. Many factors besides the Expression Number enter into our abilities and there are many inter-relation-

* My Scotty's "given" name is Jane (6 Soul Urge, 3 Expression); her pet name is Boo-Boo (6 Soul Urge, 1 Expression) and she is truly the pivot around which everything swings in my household.

ships that must be considered. For instance, the sum of the letters of the *first* name is our Key—that which enables us to "unlock" the various experiences we meet with; we may not like the *sound* of our Key, but we must consider its *number* when we change our name. The first *letter* of the first name is the *Cornerstone*—that upon which we are built and which supports our entire structure; we have already noted some instances of its importance in the Bible references.

On the Life Path we are subject to different influences at different times in the Cycles and Pinnacles* and we must know just which ones are operating at the moment.

We may be entirely lacking in certain vibrations and these are our "Karmic Lessons";* if we can supply these in the new name we may make them our servants and cease to be their slaves.

It is easy to see, then, the necessity for consulting a good "doctor" if the old infirmities are to be corrected and no new diseases acquired.

Many people have changed their entire lives by changing their names—attracting to their Paths a Market for their wares, an audience for their utterances, and money, freedom and success for their new activities.

Samuel Langhorne Clemens, for example, was just as good a writer before he took the nom de plume Mark Twain, but the original Samuel was hidden away behind the 2 of his name-total. His 22 Life Path, giving him the opportunity of masterful accomplishment through labor, might have held back its more spectacular rewards if the light of 11 had not lent its rays to attract the fame to which he was entitled. Again, a 2 Expression on a 22

* See Part 2.

Path is like trying to make a new ocean by putting in a drop of water at a time; the *material* may be there but the spiggot is too small to let it out in one short lifetime.

$$
\begin{array}{ccccc}
\underline{9} & + & \underline{12-3} & + & \underline{10-1} \quad =4 \text{ Soul Urge} \\
\end{array}
$$

		1 3 5		1	6	5		5	5		
	S A M U E L		L A N G H O R N E				C L E M E N S				
	1 4	3	3 5 7 8	9 5				3 3	4	5 1	

$$
\underline{8} \quad + \quad \underline{37-1} \quad + \quad \underline{16-7} \quad =7 \text{ Quiescent Self}
$$

1 1 4 3 5 3   3 1 5 7 8 6 9 5 5   3 3 5 4 5 5 1

$$
\underline{17-8} \quad + \quad \underline{49-4} \quad + \quad \underline{26-8} \quad = 2 \text{ Expression}
$$

$$
\begin{array}{ccc}
\underline{1} & + & \underline{10-1} \\
\end{array} = 2 \text{ Soul Urge}
$$

	1				1	9	
M	A	R	K	T	W	A	I	N
4	9	2		2	5			5

$$
\underline{15-6} \quad + \quad \underline{12-3} \quad = \quad 9 \text{ Quiescent Self}
$$

4 1 9 2   2 5 1 9 5

$$
\underline{16-7} \quad + \quad \underline{22} \quad = 7-22 = 11 \text{ Expression}
$$

Born November 30th 1835
11 + 3 + 8 = 22 Life Path

Sarah Bernhardt is another example of the strong light of a new 11. As Rosine Bernard she expressed 7—a number unfriendly to the glare of the footlights (although a fine acting vibration for *screen* artists). With the new name she did not change her original Soul Urge—8—but she helped herself to give to the world the Illumination (11) of which she was capable by selecting the brilliant 11. She thus gained for herself the logical reward of her Path of Hard Work (4) and lifted her own opportunities to the nth dimension.

```
        2         +              6              =8  Soul Urge
  ────────────  ────────────────────────────
    1   1         5       1
  S A R A H   B E R N H A R D T
  1   9   8   2   9 5 8     9 4 2
  ──────────  ──────────────────────
      18−9     +          39−3            =3  Quiescent Self
  ──────────  ──────────────────────
  1 1 9 1 8   2 5 9 5 8 1 9 4 2
  ──────────  ──────────────────────
      20−2     +          45−9            =11 Expression


        20−2      +              6              =8  Soul Urge
  ────────────  ────────────────────────────
    6   9   5     5       1
  R O S I N E   B E R N A R D
  9   1     5   2   9 5     9 4
  ──────────  ──────────────────────
      15−6     +          29−11           =8  Quiescent Self
  ──────────  ──────────────────────
  9 6 1 9 5 5 + 2 5 9 5 1 9 4
  ──────────  ──────────────────────
      35−8     +          35−8            =7  Expression
```

(It might be in order to remark at this point that, 11 and 22, the Master Numbers, should be *assumed* only when the individual feels that he is capable of great and selfless accomplishment. These numbers are of tremendous voltage and are a great tax upon the one who bears them. If they are yours originally, know that you *have* the power to live up to their requirements. They do not always spell fame and fortune, but sometimes only unbalance and defeat.)

Mary Pickford, as Gladys Smith, was already expressing 11, but "Gladys Smith" does not lend itself to electric lights, because of its looks and its sound, and MARY PICKFORD, with 5 in the Soul and 4 in Expression (with a 1-3 behind it) seems to have gained everything one small person should reasonably expect from life.

```
        8        +        9        =8  Soul Urge
      ─────────────    ─────────────
         1   7              9
    G  L  A  D  Y  S    S  M  I  T  H
    7  3     4     1    1  4     2  8
      ─────────────    ─────────────
          15—6      +      15—6       =3  Quiescent Self
      ─────────────    ─────────────
    7  3  1  4  7  1    1  4  9  2  8
      ─────────────    ─────────────
          23—5      +      24—6       =11 Expression


         8       +        15—6       =5 Soul Urge
      ─────────    ──────────────────
         1   7         9        6
    M  A  R  Y    P  I  C  K  F  O  R  D
    4  9          7  3  2  6     9  4
      ─────────    ──────────────────
         13—4    +        31—4        =8 Quiescent Self
      ─────────    ──────────────────
    4  1  9  7    7  9  3  2  6  6  9  4
      ─────────    ──────────────────
         21—3    +        46—1        =4 Expression
```

There is a large army of authors, actors, musicians and painters who have made their "fame and fortune" through adopted names—some as the direct result of the counsel of the Numerologist, others for various reasons of their own—but who is to say that the change of vibration has not been the largest contributing factor in their success? Rebecca West, Leopold Stokowski, Neysa Mc-Mein, Ann Harding, Maude Adams, Douglas Fairbanks, Ina Claire and Erich Maria Remarque are a few of the shining examples.

If you have the problem of public life before you, a writing career or a new line of development which you mean to follow, look carefully at your name and see if it *fits*. If it doesn't and you *want* it changed, have it done, by all means. It will undoubtedly bring you much outward opportunity. Let no one persuade you into it, however, for it will do you no good unless it is your own desire and impulse. At any rate, it will take the better part of a year for it to become established as a part of your own vibration.

Names assumed through marriage or adoption are again "angles of development." With marriage new vibrations, new ties and a new environment are usually acquired; you will assume other interests and responsibilities and a new set of adjustments ready for you to handle. If the new name isn't what you want it to express, change it to fit the new situation—always considering your own unchangeable conditions. Sometimes a change in spelling or the addition of a middle name or initial is all that is necessary.

Your signature is another point to be considered. Perhaps it is all wrong for the type of work you are doing and is creating an impression that is hindering you. What you *naturally* assume usually has substantial reason behind it and as we progress in life there is a tendency to drop the vibrations with which we have finished. The outstanding figures in the world are frequently known by a single name—having discarded all superfluous baggage and vibrating at last to the one thing for which they stand—as Shakespeare, 9; Napoleon, 11; Edison, 3; Ford, 7; Ghandi—another kind of 7; Byrd, 22.

If the circumstances warrant it, much can be *alleviated* by a change of name, and while the stronger ones will perhaps choose to work out their problems regardless of handicaps, we are all entitled to any legitimate help we can get—providing it does no violence to the purpose of our Being. There are countless vibrations given us to work with; let us choose wisely and then help ourselves to them.

CHAPTER VI

UNIVERSAL VIBRATIONS

THIS is the way the whole world is going—and ourselves along with it. It is a general trend that is determined by universal laws and is *indicated* by the numbers we find on the calendar. The character of this trend changes every twelve months and with the coming in of each new year, we have a different vibration to respond to.

September, of each year, since it is the 9th month, begins to "finish" the influence that has prevailed since January 1st and to forecast the one of the new year; it is "on the cusp"—not quite through with the old, not yet assuming the new, but giving us a combination of both. From then on, until the 31st of December, the old vibration grows weaker and the new one stronger, until the old year is finally seen "out" and the new one ushered in on its own feet.

HOW TO FIND THE UNIVERSAL YEAR

Add together the separate numbers or digits of the calendar year.

For example: This is the calendar year 1931.

$$
\begin{array}{r}
\text{Adding} \quad 1 \\
9 \\
3 \\
1 \\
\hline
\end{array}
$$

We have, as a result, 14

Reducing 14 to a single digit, we have as a result (1+4=)5—the Universal Year number of 1931. (See the Table of Universal Years.)

To find the vibration for *any* year, we use the same process as we did for 1931, adding the single numbers together and reducing to a final digit—(except when the sum is 11 or 22). Thus, if we want to know what kind of a year it was when Columbus discovered America, we set up 1492 in the same manner as we did 1931:

Adding   1
          4
          9
          2
          —
We have, as a result,   16

Reducing 16 to a final digit (1+6=7) we find 7 to be the Universal Year vibration for 1492.

If we want to find the vibration-number of the year in which the last war occurred, we set up 1914 as above and learn that the sum is 15 or 6—and thus for any desired year.

TABLE OF UNIVERSAL YEARS

Below are the types of things we may expect to find the world interested in or active about when each vibration is in force.

IN A 1-YEAR

Invention	New Ventures
Exploration	Progressive Plans
Creative Activity	Feats of Daring

Every year which adds to 10 (1) marks a new era of events. In 1927 we had the first successful pioneer flight across the Atlantic.

In 1926 the world wasn't ready for it—but it was not to wait until 1928. The 1-vibration of 1927 gave the necessary impetus.

IN A 2-YEAR

Collection
Arrangement
Work in Association
Efforts toward Peace between Nations
Political Discussion
Statistics and Information
Maintenance of Institutions
Drawing up of Agreements

In 1928 the Kellogg Peace Pact was signed.

IN A 3-YEAR

Expression and Activity on the Lighter Side
Expansion for Theatres and Places of Amusement
Expenditure of Money and Effort in all Directions
Restlessness
Scattering of Forces—to the point of recklessness
Demand for Pleasure and Luxury

1929 was a great year for sports and clothes, for grand pianos and motor cars. Many "fliers" were taken in securities—with crashing results in the stock market.

IN A 4-YEAR

WORK

Getting down to brass tacks. After a general shaking-up, affairs must assume their level—slowly but surely, and as a result of flying too high, things fall *hard* and first strike *below* the level. We were reminded, in 1930 that a secure foundation is vital to lasting success—and the whole year said—BUILD IT.

1930 saw many men and women getting down to work of a more or less grinding type. Wages were not quite so high because there wasn't as much available money to pay them—but then, neither were rents, for many families doubled up under one roof and hung out the TO LET sign on the old apartment. Neither were jobs as easy to find, for the boss was doing much of the work himself. Along with the other building, however, came progress in education and manufacturing—and a welcome return to some of the beautiful handcraft which gets lost in the machinery of swifter-moving years. The solid things had their "innings."

In a 5-Year

Activity in commerce and international trade
Better working conditions
Interest in new and varied subjects
Concern with Metaphysics
Commercial Psychology
Urge toward rejuvenation

As soon as the "scare" of last year is dispelled, the universal nose will lift itself from the grindstone and seek to expand its own interests and enterprises. Renewed youth will flow in business and physical veins. We shall soon be ready to "take a chance" again.

In a 6-Year

Adjustment and Harmonization
International Responsibilities Considered
Movements for Improved Health Conditions
Advance in Education
Home Economics

Marriage-license bureaus usually have to increase their staffs in a 6-year, or work over-time to take care of the applications. Marriage is in the air. After so much breathless activity, the world wants to settle down.

General adjustment and harmonization becomes of paramount importance and if things have gone too far in the 5-year to make it peaceably possible, War usually takes a hand so that the job may be thoroughly done.

Locally, many clubs and societies are formed for "village improvement," homes are redecorated and replenished. Comfort and improvement come to the fore.

IN A 7-YEAR

PERFECTING

A good financial year except when the previous one has spelled War. The farmer should come into his own, for 7 loves the country and agricultural pursuits. The vibration says Perfection, so the tendency will be to give a finished quality to everything undertaken. It is a fertile soil for the growth of theories, but takes a lot of quiet *thinking* to keep them healthy. Mining stocks should climb. Waterways should be repaired. *Existing* affairs should be analyzed. No branching out into new ventures.

7 is an Inner Force and lends itself to acquaintanceship with hidden and interior conditions.

IN AN 8-YEAR

Prosperity and Expansion

Huge amalgamations

Business increase and activity

Commercial relations with foreign countries

Engineering

This is the vibration for the turning of wheels and the speeding up of machinery. Power and Big Affairs prevail. Thinking is done in large terms and business expands and increases. Output and intake assume large proportions. Commerce extends its boundaries. Foreign trade makes a record. In 1934 the Engineers should do something to startle the world.

IN A 9-YEAR

THE CHALLENGER

The Great Challenger comes in a 9-year. Selfishness and greed cannot flourish and if indulged in, turn themselves into smashing boomerangs. The vibration says Love and Brotherhood. This is the end of a Cycle. Hatred and bitterness are to be tied in a bundle and dropped into the sea. Odds and ends of unsatisfactory relationships are to be finished up. A general housecleaning is to be given to all departments.

This is a Friendship Year—one of love, tolerance, understanding, "live and let live." Many things are "lost" in the 9. The Universe keeps on growing and has no time nor room for the old, the finished and the outworn.

IN AN 11-YEAR

THE IDEALIST

Matters of religion come to the fore. Teachers of psychology spring up like mushrooms and all their classes are crowded. Much interest is shown in Spiritualism and all forms of Occultism. Dreamers of dreams expound their theories from soap-boxes—and everybody listens and thinks it over. Old inspirational inventions are dusted off and reconsidered. New ones are dreamed about—for the betterment of mankind. Business conditions may not be improved, but resolutions are made to put them on a more altruistic basis (which may improve them later) and the revivalist, in all departments, reaps a harvest.

Our last 11-year was 1910; our next will be 2009, so some of us may not be here to receive its benefits.

IN A 22-YEAR

THE MASTER BUILDER

Another year of expansion and Big Things—now permeated with big purposes and high concepts. There is an atmosphere not only of business but of Greatness, a tremendous materialistic force that is humanitarian. Many projects will be launched that will be of general, instead of localized benefit. We shall find in the air an impetus toward world betterment; we shall *see* the practical expression of this impetus.

CHAPTER VII

HOW TO FIND THE UNIVERSAL MONTH

ADD the number of the *calendar* month to the Universal Year.

JANUARY is the 1st month, therefore its number is....1
FEBRUARY is the 2nd month, "   "   "   " 2
MARCH is the 3rd month, "   "   "   " 3
APRIL is the 4th month, "   "   "   " 4
MAY is the 5th month, "   "   "   " 5
JUNE is the 6th month, "   "   "   " 6
JULY is the 7th month, "   "   "   " 7
AUGUST is the 8th month, "   "   "   " 8
SEPTEMBER is the 9th month, "   "   "   " 9
OCTOBER is the 10th month, "   "   "   " 1
NOVEMBER is the 11th month, "   "   "   " ....2 (or 11)
DECEMBER is the 12th month, "   "   "   " 3

Suppose we want to find the vibration for May, 1931. We know that May's number is 5; we know that 1931's number is 5.

Adding 5 (for May)
and   5 (for 1931)
        ——

We get, as a result, 10, or 1—the Universal Month vibration for May, 1931.

Any other month in this year or any other may be found in the same manner—that is, by adding the calendar *number* of the month, to the Universal number of the year.

For example: We want the vibration for the *month* in which Columbus discovered America—October, 1492.

Adding   1 (for October)
and   7 (for 1492)

We get, as a result, 8—the Universal Month vibration for October, 1492.

Table of Universal Months

Universal Months will necessarily be influenced by the Universal Year, but each month, through its own vibration, will give a different angle or impetus to the general trend.

In a 1-Month

New Ideas set forth. Leaders appointed. New Committees formed.

In a 2-Month

Materials *collected*. Statistics compiled. Politics juggled.

In a 3-Month

Activity in the Market. *Operating* Committees. Amusements.

In a 4-Month

Mistakes corrected. Exactness demanded. Skilled workers called in. Slow and careful building for ultimate service.

In a 5-Month

Increase of sales. Speculation. Spurt in advertising. Unusual projects and articles placed on the market. Activity in the theatres.

IN A 6-MONTH

Community needs. Weddings. Civic improvements. Education. Health. Balance.

IN A 7-MONTH

Improved finances. Invention. Examination and analysis.

IN AN 8-MONTH

Substantial expansion. Growth. Large plans put into action. Organizations formed for business promotion.

IN A 9-MONTH

Inventories. Elimination. Public characters to the fore.

IN AN 11-MONTH

Activity among Evangelists. Cults. Churches and Missions.

IN A 22-MONTH

Civic and national projects for improved conditions. Railroads. Waterways. International relationships.

CHAPTER VIII

KNOW THE UNIVERSAL DAY

SINCE the vibrations change every twenty-four hours, each day has an influence of its own. To find this we learn first the Universal Year (by adding together the digits of the calendar year); add to that the calendar Month (as January 1, February 2, etc.) and then add to these two the calendar Day (as 1st, 3rd, etc.).

For example:—To find the Universal Day vibration on the anniversary of Lincoln's birthday (Feb. 12th) in 1931.

Adding.... 5 (the Universal Year in 1931)
and   .... 2 (the calendar month of February)
and   .... 3 (12 reduced to a single digit)
—
Result ....10 or 1—The Universal Day Number of Lincoln's birthday in 1931.

To find the Universal Day vibration when the Declaration of Independence was signed—July 4, 1776.

Adding the digits of 1776 we get.... 3—Universal Year in 1776
Adding the calendar Month (July)... 7
Adding the calendar Day (4th)...... 4
—
Result ....14 = 5—the Universal Day vibration when the Declaration of Independence was signed.

TABLE OF UNIVERSAL DAYS

WHAT TO EXPECT

ON A 1-DAY

Efforts to promote new ideas. Strong market. Strikes.

On a 2-Day

Inertia. Increase of death notices. Quiet. Accumulation.

On a 3-Day

Activity. Restlessness. Nervous energy. Scattered forces. Erratic market.

On a 4-Day

Hum of machinery. Detail. Attention to schedule. Steadier market.

On a 4-Day also, there is often increase of illness and death. There may be evidences of anarchy (strikes, demonstrations, rebellion), owing to the fact that 4 clamps down the lid and, if other influences have caused seething conditions below the surface, the lid may blow off.

On a 5-Day

Pleasure. Freedom. Curiosity. Speculation. Epidemics. Large attendance at the theatres and restaurants.

On a 6-Day

Restaurants less crowded. Concerts well attended. Stocks more adjusted.

The Universe eats at home but goes to a concert, or turns on the radio.

On a 7-Day

Improvements in the market. Perfecting of fine points. Analysis. In the cities—irritation and lack of poise. In the country, peace and quiet.

On an 8-Day

Big deals put through. Directors' meetings. Bustling executives.

On a 9-Day

Public affairs considered. More tolerance. Friendly relations.

> All 2-Days may have the spirit of 11.
> All 4-Days may have the spirit of 22.

Universal Trends as Reflected in History

1 Vibration

1927 $(1 + 9 + 2 + 7 = 1)$. A pioneer year for the establishment of new airplane records. Chamberlain, Byrd and Lindbergh all made their flights in this year. A new standard was established, a former dream accomplished, a new era of progress begun. The spirit of the year was creative. The men who expressed the spirit had every quality of the constructive 1. They sought what they wanted and got it—for the world.

2 Vibration

1928 $(1 + 9 + 2 + 8 = 2)$. The Briand-Kellogg treaty to end war was signed by representatives of fifteen nations. Diplomacy, harmony, poise, receptivity and balance accomplished what would have been a hopeless task for the spirit of adventure. Knowledge, friendliness and peace were gained by this great Act.

3 Vibration

1929 $(1 + 9 + 2 + 9 = 3)$. Truly a year of Expression. Plays and concerts, clothes and amusements, entertainment and extravagance were the order of the day. The hour of reckoning, when hopes and plans and paper houses came crashing suddenly to earth, hit only those who had flown too far and had forgotten the gas for the engine—like the unfortunate biblical virgins who neglected to put the oil in their lamps. Those who have not lived true to the 1 and the 2 are not ready for the 3.

4 Vibration

1876 $(1 + 8 + 7 + 6 = 4)$. The first telephone patent was taken out by Alexander Bell—a perfect example of slow and careful building expressed in permanent and useful terms.

5 Vibration

July 4th, 1776 $(7 + 4 + 1 + 7 + 7 + 6 = 5)$. It needs no analysis to fit the spirit of this day with 5. Freedom and fearlessness, adventure and keen outlook, enthusiasm and the grasp of opportunity found their expression in this act of independence. The 3-vibration of the year added its influence of New Joy in Living.

6 Vibration

Adjustment! Sometimes through war, sometimes through peace—but always with the end in view of restoring the true level.

1905 $(1 + 9 + 0 + 5 = 6)$. Japan and Russia agreed to President Roosevelt's request to discuss peace terms. The agreement was ratified.

1914 $(1 + 9 + 1 + 4 = 6)$. Austria-Hungary declared war against Servia—thus beginning an adjustment so far-reaching and uprooting that it carried over into the 7, 8 and 9 and past the zenith of the 1-year (in the 9th month of the 1-year) when the foreshadowing of the more kindly and harmonious 2 was beginning to make itself felt. Not until then could peace be established.

(N.B. The Armistice was signed in an 11-month.)

7 VIBRATION

Outstanding events are not usual in the 7-year. The influence is usually static and its effect interior. Irritation is apt to express itself in disputes *within* nations rather than *between* them—keeping evidences of bad temper in the family instead of seeking the open. Many local battles—even massacres of whole villages—have occurred in 7-years; also religious disputes and persecutions in the name of theology and dogma. In the United States the famous trial of Aaron Burr took place in a 7-year (1807) and much controversy over rights and principles has been held in similar years in other countries. The tendency is always toward the non-spectacular; any development is apt to be of slow growth and any explosion local. It is a good financial year for those who are willing to work and analyze. Much attention is focussed upon *water* (the Element of 7). Improvements in waterways, strengthening of dams and long water journeys occupy the public mind. (Columbus discovered America in a 7-year.)

8 VIBRATION

This year marks the expression of the accumulated irritations of the 7. The United States declared war on Spain in 1898 (an 8-year). It is also, on its happier side, a great year for progress and prosperity. As long ago as 1763 (an 8-year) the first balloon ascension was made with heated air, and every 8-year since that time has been outstanding in material progress. Our next 8-year will be in 1934 and what we are likely to see is beyond the realm of prophecy.

9 VIBRATION

THE FINISHER

1701 $(1 + 7 + 0 + 1 = 9)$. Captain Kidd was hanged in England.

December 13, 1865 $(3 + 4 + 1 + 8 + 6 + 5 = 27 = 9)$. This marked the ratification of the 13th Amendment to the Constitution of the United States, abolishing slavery for all time.

1917 $(1 + 9 + 1 + 7 = 18 = 9)$. The United States severed diplomatic relations with Germany (on February 3rd—a 5-vibration) and entered the World War the same year (on April 6th, a 1-vibration).

1926 $(1 + 9 + 2 + 6 = 18 = 9)$. The National Broadcasting Company completed its organization to give to the world chain-radio programs.

11 VIBRATION

1712 $(1 + 7 + 1 + 2 = 11)$. Frederick the Great was born—an idealist and a man of vision, whatever we may think of his policies or their results in Prussian Militarism.

1802 $(1 + 8 + 0 + 2 = 11)$. Washington, D. C., was incorporated as a city. The original intention surely was to "follow the star." Our next 11-year will be in 2009, but in November of every year we find the 11-vibration in the calendar Month, and may use it if we will.

22 VIBRATION

FOR THE GOOD OF THE WORLD

1777 $(1 + 7 + 7 + 7 = 22)$. Congress adopted the Stars and Stripes as the national flag.

1858 $(1 + 8 + 5 + 8 = 22)$. The first trans-Atlantic cable was laid. These are two great examples of practical idealism.

The inspiration for accomplishment!
The vision in working form!

CHAPTER IX

YOUR PERSONAL YEAR

ALWAYS consider the Universal Year before making conclusions about your own *Personal* Year—then WORK YOUR OWN.

We must all take the general direction of the Universe, but our own relation to it is a purely personal and individual matter. You will be conscious of the prevailing influences that affect everybody and will yourself feel hampered or encouraged by them, as the case may be, but whatever the Universal vibration is, if it differs from your own Personal Year, its influence does not and should not submerge your own number. Your numbers, like any other personal property, belong to *you* and for your own best good and progress you should consciously put yourself into their current that they may help to carry you along.

If you find yourself obliged to live in an ugly town where no one is making any effort to beautify his house or grounds, that does not mean that *your* house must be unbeautiful or that *you* cannot have a lovely garden—if you take the trouble to plant it and care for it. Or if, in 1930, when the Universal vibration said Work and Limitation, your Personal Year happened to say Travel, that did not mean that you had to do the same type of grinding that your neighbor did, but that your opportunity was to be found by taking trips away from your shop or desk; *you* were given more freedom because *your* year said Keep Moving: you had to work (or at least to feel the general limitation from some angle) but you weren't confined to the square of the 4.

To keep "in tune" you must *take* the Universal, or general direction and then *do* the things your *personal* vibrations indicate.

To Find Your Personal Year

First find the number of the Universal Year (see Chapter 6). You cannot get your own until you know the Universal.

Your Personal Year is the number of the Universal *plus* your own *birth month and day.*

If you were born in January, add 1 for your month; if in February, add 2, etc., then add the digit or final figure of the *day* of the month—your birthday.

For example: Your birthday is August 5th and you want to find your Personal Year for 1931.

Add together August (the 8th month)....... 8
your birthday (the 5th).................. 5
and the Universal Year in 1931............ 5
                                         —
The sum of these is......................18
and the final reduction (1 + 8 = 9) is 9—your Personal
    Year in 1931.

Or:

Suppose we would like to know what kind of a Personal Year the Mayor of New York City had when he was re-elected to office in 1929.

James Joseph Walker was born on June 19th. By add-

ing together the digits of 1929, we find that it was a 3
Universal Year.

Adding together June (the 6th month)...... 6
and the Mayor's birthday (19th)......... 1
and the Universal Year in 1929.......... 3

We get the result of...............10 or 1.

Turning to the Table of Personal Years for the meaning
of 1, we may conclude that the vibration helped him to
get something for himself.
Again:

Alfred Emanuel Smith was born on December 3rd.
His Personal vibration in 1929 told a different story.

Adding together December (the 12th month)... 3
and the former Governor's birthday....... 3
and the Universal Year in 1929.......... 3

We get the result of.............. 9

Turning to the Table of Personal Years, we learn that
9 is a year in which to finish up the old and not take on
the new. It was not a propitious year for starting a new
enterprise. Any form of activity *begun* in a 9-year will
not last, and if Mr. Smith had been elected to the Presi-
dency, circumstances would undoubtedly have so shaped
themselves as to make his tenure of office of very short
duration. In other words—it would have finished itself.

TABLE OF PERSONAL YEARS

1-YEAR

Individualize yourself in every way. Hold fast to your
own ideals and purposes. Be independent and follow your
own counsel—first making sure you are right. Go straight

on and don't turn aside for things or people. Hold a listening ear—but for the voice within instead of without. Make the change you were contemplating; promote your new scheme or make some addition to your present line. You are at the turn of the road; change is in the air. This is the opportunity you have been waiting for— for the past nine years. You are at your height of power. This is your *planting* time. Hold a constant picture of the thing you want to be doing and the person you want to be at the close of the next nine years. Plant the *kind* of seed you want to see come up. Whatever you sow *now* you will reap later. Above all else—*don't be lazy!*

2-Year

This year the seeds you planted in the "1" will germinate. This is a time not so much for action as for attraction. Things will come to you if you are quiet and receptive. You are ready for accumulation. Keep an open mind. Study all you can and acquire new information on the subject which interests you the most. Plan to work with others instead of trying to go it alone. Keep calm and cool and pleasant. Strengthen your friendships. Keep your goal in mind and *collect* things that will help you to reach it. New opportunities and privileges will drop into your lap if you don't make too much effort to seek them. Be patient. Don't expect to see any results from last year's planting. Fertilize the soil and wait for things to grow below the surface. Don't be sensitive. Do the *small* things. WAIT.

3-Year

This is the year for you to cultivate the society of your old friends and make new ones. Plan to do a lot of entertaining and accept invitations. The conditions around you are cheerful and optimistic. You will not be overburdened with responsibilities and may safely take some time off to enjoy yourself. You may have a tendency to scatter your energies and undertake too many things at a time, so be careful to finish one thing before starting another. Be happy, but don't give yourself over to frivolity. You may hold fast to a Purpose and still not be overshadowed by gloom. Some of the flowers planted in the 1-Year should begin to show their heads. Enjoy them. You are in a halo of light, art, beauty; let others enjoy it.

4-Year

This is your year to work. If you are too easy on yourself, or do too much loafing, you will probably suffer in health so you won't get much satisfaction out of your leisure. You must dig and hoe and cultivate and build if you want to have a real vacation next year. Test everything for practicality and stability. Square up past mistakes and figure out how to avoid new ones. Work out all the details of that project you have been turning over in your mind; strengthen all its weak places. Put all your affairs in perfect order. Look well to your health—especially in matters of diet. Be sane and rational in all things. KEEP BUSY.

5-Year

This year you should feel as free as the air—to go where you please; but, by all means, go *somewhere,* for your opportunity will be found outside the ordinary routine. Let go of many old things and make room for new ones. Welcome new situations, places and people.

This is a year of progress. If you have a business of your own, present it with a new angle. Do a lot of advertising. Don't let the prevailing atmosphere of change and variety make you restless—take advantage of it to learn something new. Don't scatter yourself and burn up all your energies; let your adaptability keep the balance between concentration and explosion. Do a variety of things, but let each one be of use to you. GET OUT OF THE RUT.

6-Year

This year you have more responsibility than you had in the "5". Don't plan to be too personal, for you will be needed in many directions and will be called upon to make adjustments for those less able to do so than you are. Narrow yourself down a bit and plan to enjoy your home life. You will be surrounded by love and friendliness and contentment—if you allow yourself to attract them. Be very thorough and conscientious about everything you do, *finishing* all you undertake. Don't hustle or bustle—just ease things into the places that fit them. It isn't a year for big accomplishment and things may seem to be at a standstill, but the Law is working unceasingly and making many unseen adjustments in your own life. It is the most personal of all the vibrations and "what is mine shall see my face." A fine and friendly influence for marriage and all home conditions.

7-Year

This is the year for the spiritual hen to sit upon her nest—not a happy time for social activities or too much association with crowds. Plan to spend a good deal of time alone and get acquainted with your powers, past mistakes and future desires. Don't *brood* over the past—simply look it over and put it where it belongs. Let everything pertaining to business remain where it is. It is not a time for expansion or change—only for reflection and perfection. Analyze everything you have or are doing. Deepen the roots of everything that is worth keeping. It is a good financial vibration if we don't strain after money for its material uses. Await developments.

8-Year

This is your power year. Now is the time to make great forward strides. Through work, effort and activity you put yourself under the Law of Compensation and should now see much of the fruit of your planting. Activity is your keynote—the whole world is your field. Gather all your forces together and branch out. Plan, think and *act*. Compel things to come to you and to work for you. Deal out full measure of justice in everything you do. There are big things to be done and big opportunities for their doing. Power is in the air—for YOU.

9-Year

This is the time to WEED the garden—at home, in business or personal relationships. It is not always an easy year, for the old stumbling-blocks will appear unexpectedly upon the path and if you don't take the trouble to roll them out of the way, they will trip you up and maybe *lay* you up. Things that have been lagging behind must be finished up this year and all accounts "paid in full". DO IT NOW—it mustn't be carried over. You will find

the year full of love and happiness if you don't make of
yourself the center of the Universe. This is a friendship
year, but it is also the time to take the inventory. You are
in process of completion, the preparation for a new "beginning of 9". Cultivate music, writing, nature and the
arts; express love to the many and toleration to all.
Finish up and throw out all that has delayed or hampered
you.

11-Year

This is another "inner year"—like the 7. This is the
time for the ideals to light up whatever we do. Its only
concern is with inside growth; it checks us up on the
principles we have been using—in business or with
people. If we start at the bottom and see that everything
is sound and spotless, we are likely to be guided into the
right moves—externals won't be able to turn us aside. If
we don't bother much about it, however, we are likely
to drop into the negative 2—and be blocked and limited.
Our attention is likely to be called to many religious and
psychic matters during the year and we may acquire a
new type of illumination to pass on to others.

22-Year

This is the year to put dreams to practical use. The
vibration belongs to humanity at large and has little personal concern. We may find ourselves the chief instigators
or chief actors, but our motives are for general instead
of personal advancement—if we are to reap the many
benefits of the influence. Put on full steam and don't
allow yourself to be thwarted. This is your chance to do
something big for the good of the world.

Tides of the Years

When you are active, seeking, expressing and achieving, your "tides" are "in". Things are moving with and for you. You can see the results of your activities and may expect responses to your efforts.

When you are waiting, perfecting, reflecting and keeping quiet, your tides are "out". Things may be moving toward you just the same, but the accumulation is for the future and not for immediate use.

In a 1-Year........Your tide is in.
" " 2- " ....Your tide is out.
" " 3- " ....Your tide is in.
" " 4- " ....Your tide is out.
" " 5- " ....Your tide is in.
" " 6- " ....Your tide is out.
" " 7- " ....Your tide is *way* out.
" " 8- " ....Your tide is *way* in.
" " 9- " ....Your tide is in and out—
          "on the cusp".
" " 11- " ....Your tide is out.
" " 22- " ....Your tide is in—
          for humanity.

CHAPTER X

YOUR PERSONAL MONTH

AFTER finding the Universal Year and then your Personal Year, learn the numbers of your Personal *Months* and let the type of thing you do each month take on the color of the governing vibration of your *own* month.

To find your Personal Month—

Add your *Personal* Year to the *Calendar* Month.

For example:

Suppose that your Personal Year is 6 and you want to know what kind of a month you will have in July.

Add together July (the 7th month)........ 7
and your Personal Year................ 6
                                            —
You find, as a result................ 13 or 4—

the number of your Personal Month in July. Consult the Table of Personal Months to learn what you should do in July—and, by the same process, in any other month in your 6 Personal Year.

You have probably noticed that the number 9, when added to or subtracted from any other number, does not alter the final digit of the result. Therefore September, being the 9th month, will have the same *month* vibration as the *year*. For example: 1931 is a 5-Year (Universal) September is the 9th month:

Add together September (the 9th month).... 9
and the Universal Year in 1931.......... 5

We get, as a result................14 or 5—

which is the same number as the Universal Year. This means that every September gives us a "double dose" of the vibration that prevails for the year. Everything is intensified along the lines of the meaning of the number —and it hits the hardest just as it is about to relinquish its hold, or begins to *finish* the old vibration and take on the influence of the new. This holds good in the Personal vibration as well as the Universal.

TABLE OF PERSONAL MONTHS

1-MONTH

Action, Creation, Seeking the New, Making Changes. The *Start*.

Negative—Laziness, Apathy, Discouragement; or Self-insistence and Pugnacity.

2-MONTH

Rest, Harmony, Sound Friendships, Peace-making, Service, Accumulation, Study.

Negative—Moodiness, Indifference, Over-Sensitiveness, Discontent, Slackness.

3-MONTH

Expressing the Talents, Promoting Social Activity, Having a Good Time.

Negative—Whining, Scattering, Encouraging Gossip, Restlessness, Nervousness, Extravagance.

4-Month

Directed Effort, Skilled Work, Service, Organization.
Negative—Promoting Strife, Refusing to Work, Creating Disorder, Feeling Limitation.

5-Month

Advertising, Promotion, Expansion, Freedom, Untried Ventures, New Things and People.
Negative—Eternal Pleasure-Seeking, Confusion, Staying in the Rut.

6-Month

Harmony at Home, Responsibility, Balance, Music, Beauty, Happiness, Family.
Negative—Refusing to make Adjustments, Unwillingness to meet Obligations, Meddlesomeness, Imposition of Personal Standards.

7-Month

Silence, Patience, Perfecting of the Thing in Hand, Self-Examination, Mental Analysis, WAITING.
Negative—Seeking to Improve Material Conditions, Impatience, Secretiveness.

8-Month

Power, Fearlessness, Good Judgment, Constructive Expansion, Material Freedom.
Negative—Lack of Vision, Centering on Detail, Recklessness, Abuse of Power.

9-MONTH

Broad Outlook, Impersonal Love, Service to the Many, Expression in Higher Art-Forms, Concern for Humanity, Public Performances.

Negative—Centering on the Self, Neglecting Friendships, Narrowing the Interests.

11-MONTH

Spiritual Vision, Expression of Ideals, Religion, Higher Thought, Launching the Invention, Psychology, Interest in General Welfare and Social Betterment.

Negative—Penuriousness, Self-interest, Hoarding, Irritability, Impracticality.

22-MONTH

Putting the Ideals to Work, Service to the All, Launching of Huge Projects, International Concern, Material Mastery.

Negative—Stagnation, Rebellion, Misdirected Energy, Explosion.

———

The next step is to "consider your days". Always bear in mind that the vibrations change *every twenty-four hours,* and however black the skies may look today, they are sure to wear a different hue tomorrow.

CHAPTER XI

YOUR PERSONAL DAY

To find it:

> Add together Your Personal Year
> and the Calendar Month
> and the Calendar Day.

For example: Your Personal Year is 6 and you want to know what some of the national holidays will mean to *you*.

What should you do on Lincoln's Birthday, February 12th?

6	Your Personal Year
2	The Calendar number for February
(12) 3	The Calendar Day
11	Result

Turn to the Table of Personal Days (immediately following) and read both 11 and 2.

What should you do on the 4th of July?

6	Your Personal Year
7	The Calendar number for July
4	The Calendar Day
17—8	Result

Turn to the Table of Personal Days and see what an 8-day means for *you*.

You have seen that your days *are* numbered. You have learned to find out HOW.

You will discover, in the following Table, just *what to do* when each vibration comes around.

Take your own calendar and as each month comes along, mark at the top the number of your *Personal* Month (found by adding your *Personal* Year to the *Calendar* Month). This shows the kind of a month it is for *you*. Then mark *each day* (by adding its number to your Personal Month) and look up the *meaning* of the number in the Table of Personal Days. Do this the first thing each morning and see how much more easily things fall into place for you. In an incredibly short time you will find yourself adjusted to what you have to do and to what is going on around you.

Never forget the Universal vibration, which is like a TIDE that carries everybody out or in, but *remember that your own individual world is of your own making,* and that if you live "top-side" of your vibrations, you have, do and *are* everything you want.

TABLE OF PERSONAL DAYS

A 1-DAY

CREATION

START something. Make that contemplated change. Map out your plan of campaign and proceed to act upon it. Promote your own enterprises. Interview people of importance in your affairs. Seek the new job. Make appointments to discuss your own interests and take the lead in the conversation. Keep your definite purpose in mind and make every effort for its accomplishment. Do something original. Take no advice unless it appeals to your better judgment. Stand on your own feet. Trust your intuitions. Unite your thought and action. KEEP MOVING.

Today your personal power and individuality are at their height. You are independent, ambitious, energetic and self-reliant. You are headed for achievement and are not to be driven or forced from the path of progress. Your intellect is working under full steam; your judgment is excellent. You have the courage and determination to carry out your plans to a successful conclusion. You have the good sense to realize that impatience, anger, stubbornness, arrogance, selfishness, laziness, worry, anxiety or unwillingness to unite yourself with any conditions that arise would only cause you to lose control of a situation that is entirely in your own hands. Your strong-willed attitude will carry you where you want to go.

GO AFTER WHAT YOU WANT.

A 2-DAY

COLLECTION

Be receptive. Use the soft pedal on everything you do. Efface yourself and agree with your friend. Temper your own opinion to the other man's point of view. Do something for somebody. Be a go-between and peacemaker. Ask for your share of the work and say "Thank you." Mix harmoniously with others. FOLLOW—do not lead. Collect everything you can—information, new friends or things, facts; you will need a lot of material tomorrow. Keep poised, balanced, placid, good-tempered. Straighten out that misunderstanding; apologize for your fault in it —it took two to start it. Don't talk too much. Listen and think. CO-OPERATE.

Today you are the 'cello accompaniment. You don't carry the air, but you do add the harmonies that make it beautiful. You are full of sympathy and understanding—sociable and adaptable. You are glad to put everyone at ease and you have no feeling of superiority or aloofness. You are full of grace and rhythm. Being in a receptive mood, this is a day of great accumulation for you. If you do receive something today you have put yourself in contact with a current that is likely to bring things your way for the next seven days. You realize that if you are quiet and careful and pleasant you will probably get your own way—for everyone will want to give it to you. You are not really shy or negative—simply a decorative part of the background. You realize that nothing is to be gained by over-passivity, indifference or carelessness. While sensitive to the feelings and desires of others, you are not going to expose your own to be hurt. Neither will you allow yourself to be uncertain, erratic or hysterical, over-secretive or untruthful. You are going to take this opportunity to be somewhat retrospective, but not in the least melancholy. If you find yourself slipping, wear yellow and seek the sunlight.

HOLD YOUR TONGUE.
DON'T LET THE SMILE COME OFF.

A 3-DAY

EXPRESSION

Give out some of the light that floods you and vibrates around you. Start the day singing. Refuse to worry. Take everything as it comes—and like it. Don't plan ahead; get all there is out of today. Bless the first three people you see. Make play of any work that comes along. Visit your friends or entertain them—above all, entertain them, whether you visit them or not. Instead of walking, run. Work your sense of humor. Spread your gaiety and enthusiasm thick—on both sides. Sweep all obstacles before you. Laugh at failures and begin again. Put on your best clothes and go out and show everybody what an advantage there is in being beautiful. Do your shopping. If the corners of your mouth start to droop, count your blessings. Make 7 people smile—then watch your returns for seven days.

After all the riches and harmonious vibrations accumulated yesterday, you will surely burst if you don't give some of them out. You love the world and understand why so much has been said and written about the "Joy of living." If anything hits you, you can't stay down. You don't care especially about working with your hands today, for the artist in you is on top and clamoring to be recognized. You can sing, dance, play, act, speak or write. You are very independent and need nothing that you do not possess. You are not afraid of anything or anybody, for you realize that fear belongs to the mental and moral hypochondriacs—and they are welcome to it. You realize that worry, intolerance, anxiety and forebodings for the future only scatter your forces—and you have no time for them. This is another day!

LET THE LIGHT SHINE.

A 4-DAY

WORK

Get up early and plan a schedule for yourself. Use military precision in everything you do, but march (to music) from one job to the next. Obey the orders of real or fancied superiors. Live up to your plan—get everything out on time. Analyze the details and correct every error. Put yourself, your working surroundings, your correspondence and your finances *in order*. Examine the budget; see if it is keeping its symmetrical lines, or bulging in spots. Test yourself for sane economy, penuriousness or extravagance; restore the balance. Curb the flights of imagination and give a one-pointed attention to the matter in hand. Respect the conventions. Summon the determined jaw and build a lasting cornerstone.

This is the day for organization and system. You are stalwart, dependable, full of useful purpose. You are laying the foundation for your own building, so you want to be sure of the size and quality of the bricks, the stickiness of the mortar, the strength of the girders. You recognize the beauty of perfect construction, knowing that it holds the promise of definite and enduring completion. You know that four walls mean protection; that four winds of heaven have been provided for us; that there are four points to the compass; four elements; four horsemen of the Apocalypse and four sides to a perfect square. From all this, also, you know that it takes a certain kind of 4-square limitation to make freedom. You are wise enough to realize that all this toil need not mean monotony, nor the necessary plodding land you in a rut; that perfectionists are not always the best critics and that the most painstaking people need not be unduly slow.

If anyone tries to persuade you that the job is too long or too boring, refer him to Maeterlinck's "Life of the Bee."

CUT AND PRUNE AND BALANCE AND WEIGH! A LASTING TOMORROW IS FASHIONED TODAY.

A 5-DAY

EXPANSION—FREEDOM

Get away from the details. Inject new ideas into your work or plans for the day. Sharpen your curiosity about things and people in order to learn something new about them. Make as many contacts as possible. Go where you may meet strangers. Do something amusing and diverting. Welcome variety as it comes along and adapt yourself to it. Do the *same* things in a new and different way. Take a chance. Promote and advertise yourself, your business, your interests. Get a new point of view. Look at yourself and your friends from a different angle; discover new points of interest in both. Get out of the rut. See a type of play you would not ordinarily choose. Get a glimpse of a different class of people from your own. If you like fiction, read philosophy; if you are keen about ethics, read the latest detective story. Consider the causes of the differences between yourself and those you know best. Take a little time off to look UP as well as around and about. Meet any emergency and be equal to it. Exercise your versatility. Don't hide your enthusiasm. Give something away. Keep an open mind. Seize one of the opportunities that are thick about you. Keep a keen lookout.

Having properly worked your 4 yesterday, you owe yourself somewhat of a vacation today. There is an air of uncertainty about —shifting and restless—but FREE. Today you are not a specialist, rather a jack-of-all-trades; you can turn your hand to anything you like. Your mind is especially keen and you have on the tip of your tongue that bit of brilliant repartee you wanted yesterday. You are a gypsy and long for the trail; failing that, you are free to seek as much mental adventure as you please. The ominous importance of affairs is in the background and you are ready for play. You are going to take that short trip that seemed inadvisable yesterday (it probably was), for you know that today the conditions are ripe for it and you will have the outcome you are looking for. Since you are feeling like seeing people, you have decided to invite some friends in for the evening—especially those who have begun to feel neglected. You have no fears about that little "flier" in the stock market you wanted to take awhile ago. You are going to hold on to your mental equilibrium, but let go of everything else that has been keeping your nose to the grindstone. If the wife is keen about the Opera, this is a good night to try it out—it may not be such a bore after all; anyway, it will be a change. No one can prevent you from making an adventure out of the day. Your "luck" is with you and you mean to make the most of it. You have a tremendous amount of vitality and energy and general "pep," but you know better than to waste any of it in losing your temper or working up a case of nerves; it would be sure to give you indigestion if you did. You also have the good sense to realize that the kind of freedom you are after isn't to be found in the bottom of a glass, in putting your money on any old horse that is posted, or in taking the friend's best girl out to dinner. You are out for something to keep. You will know more tomorrow than you did yesterday.

> *Make a new song for a tale that is old—*
> *Blaze a new trail to a land unknown;*
> *Find a new love for your heart to hold,*
> *Open a flower as yet unblown.*

A 6-Day

ADJUSTMENT

Look at yourself. Are you brushed, in order and smart-looking? Is the color you are wearing becoming or an eye-sore? Is your mind composed and balanced so that you can listen to the hard-luck story and give advice —*if asked?* Are you shirking any responsibility that belongs to you, or assuming one that is none of your affair? Are you doing all that you should about your diet and exercise? Have you been acting a little grumpy instead of cheerful and companionable? Have you been "high-hatting" anyone from your superior heights?

Look at your surroundings. Are they in order? Are they swept and garnished? Are they as beautiful as you can make them? Do the colors clash and does the atmosphere seem unrestful and inharmonious? Have you enough comfortable chairs for your friends and clients in your office? Is your home or office running on greased wheels in every department?

Look at your family and friends. Do they need or want anything that you can provide—and haven't? Have you been holding out on money and spending too much on yourself? Is there anyone in trouble who would like your help or advice? Is anyone you know sick who would like to be visited or read to? Do you owe any calls that should be made? Any teas, luncheons or dinners that should be paid up? NOW is the time. ADJUST all along the line (wherever it is *your* line) but stifle that impulse to write a letter to the newspapers and suggest your remedies for civic wrongs; they'll only set you down as a paranoiac.

Today you are the great harmonizer and home-maker. You would like to make everybody comfortable and happy. You are a nurse, teacher, father (or mother) confessor, counsellor, refuge, asylum, host and companion—all rolled into one. If you see an urgent need for so-called physical drudgery and you seem to be the one elected to do it, you are not going to keep your mind on the soap and scrub brush, but on the shining result to be achieved. You are going to keep busy and even-tempered, but refrain from bustling about or allowing anyone to see the wheels in operation. You are going to *finish* anything you undertake, for you realize that after the 6 days everything was so complete and in order that Sunday became an institution. You are full of high principles and a great desire to adjust other lives as harmoniously as you have managed your own, but you realize the danger of becoming a meddler and busybody, and wisely decide to wait until your sympathy and advice are asked for. Your sense of duty and responsibility are at their keenest and you realize that today is the time to WORK them, for if any of the demands are neglected, you know they will rise up and smite you at a time when they would seem an impossible burden. Today it is easy. You are headed for a well-earned rest—tomorrow.

OIL THE MACHINERY.

A 7-DAY

INTROSPECTION

Take a long breath. Insist upon freedom from worry, hurry and excitement; there is an air of "Sunday" about you. Be entirely alone for a part of the day and think yourself over. Stop, look and listen. *Stop* long enough to realize that "what you shall eat and wherewithal you shall be clothed" do not constitute the whole of life or its happiness. *Look* at your sins of omission and commission and pull them up by the roots. *Listen* for the "still, small voice" that gets so little chance to be heard. Pause before you go on and realize just what you are going toward—

and why. Get into the country if possible. If not, buy yourself some flowers or take some dog out for a walk. Save a short period for absolute rest—both mental and physical. See what comes into your mind when you leave the doors open and your nerves aren't jumping about and blocking all passageways. Don't babble: *think*. Realize your poise and steadiness and quiet, but don't give the impression that you are sulky or lazy or moody. Live your own interior life and don't interfere with any one else's. Get your inspiration from Higher Up. *Seek* nothing for yourself, your family or your business. Don't try to *express*—receive impressions instead. Perfect everything you are doing—putting on all finishing touches—but don't try to make it larger or more productive. Use your *inside* power.

Since this is a day of high spiritual vibration, it is not always friendly to strictly material affairs. You will have a feeling of withdrawal from the world which you will have the good sense not to carry too far. If you want to be alone and are able to manage it, you must not spoil it all by feeling bereft and melancholy. If you are out of sympathy with what seems to be meaningless activity about you, you won't allow it to irritate or depress you, make you restless and dissatisfied or critical and intolerant. You know that you are fully capable of any effort required of you, whether you feel inclined to it or not, for your interior force and balance are seeing you through. You know that if you keep still and wait, things will come to you; if you go out after them, they will elude or disappoint you. You may be conscious of a thousand irritations, like an army of small devils, trying to throw you off your balance, but since you realize that this is a day that belongs to your interior life, you know they cannot penetrate deep enough to reach it, so you will only laugh at their antics. You are acquiring a tremendous reserve-force for tomorrow.

> *Now will I close my door and be alone,*
> *For I have need of counsel on my way.*
> *The peace of night enfolds me as I dream—*
> *I shall not heed the turmoil of the day.*

AN 8-DAY

EXECUTIVE POWER

Look to your affairs. Organize your forces. Find out just where you stand as to business or finances. Grasp the opportuinty for enlargement and do not doubt your ability to "cash in" on it. If you have already had a success, build another on top of it. Consider your chances and move forward. Realize your creative power for advancement and branch out with it. Do not speculate or fly off at tangents, but plant your feet firmly on the ground and draw all the magnetic *earth*-vibrations into your undertakings. Help yourself by helping someone less strong and powerful. Keep your *aim* in mind; use the force for material gain and advancement, in order to increase and enlarge your field of usefulness. *Drive* yourself and your affairs with confidence in a successful outcome. This is the strong arm of the material world. This is your Power-Day.

After the spiritual housecleaning of yesterday you are ready to turn your attention to purely material affairs. You realize that there is an atmosphere of worldly power and financial gain about you. Your success is in your own hands, provided you do not confuse ends and means. You are not dependent upon others but stand upon your own feet and attract their confidence by your strength. You know that money, in itself, is only a stepping-stone, and you have the clear sense and judgment to want to accumulate it for the power-for-good its possession will bring you. You want to help others as well as yourself, partly because you want to live on the constructive side of the vibration and partly because you have the intelligence to know that, of all the existing vibrations, it is the most elusive when sought for itself. Being of the earth earthy, you do not expect of it much inspiration or uplift, but you are able to endow it with those qualities which you draw from your own store, and in that way increase its power of attraction toward you. You know, too, that if you have the thing within your grasp and allow yourself to become hard and domineering, it cannot and will not remain with you, but will surely turn against you and refuse to lend a hand in your affairs. You feel the power and construction of the 4, multiplied by the kindness and beneficence of the 2; you are aware of the strength and sufficiency of the 1 added to the spiritual qualities of the 7; and you do not mean to overlook the joy-giving 3 added to the far-reaching 5, or, again, the harmonious 2 added to the adjusting 6. Taken all in all, you realize that today you are a master-mind, the true executive, dealing out justice and mercy with scientific understanding.

HIT ON ALL THE CYLINDERS.

A 9-DAY

UNIVERSALITY

Love your neighbor as yourself. Do good to "all those who despitefully use you." Read the whole Sermon on the Mount. Forget your personal desires and do some one thing that entails a sacrifice—of will or prejudice or opinion. Pull up the weeds that have been choking you. Look at everyone through rose glasses and see only their good qualities; know that those are the realities. Do that generous thing you have been hestitating about. Assume the fault in the misunderstanding of yesterday. Show your good will and bear no grudges. Do the BIG thing. Finish up all the odds and ends that have been hanging about. Cancel the date with the man who has been wasting your time. Get rid of your self-imposed conventions and limitations. Take stock of the possessions, occupations, impressions, acquaintances and pastimes that will never get you anywhere and throw them out. If you are planning a public performance, be glad it is scheduled for today. Break up all the soil around your roots. Begin to spread out and grow. Dig up your race-consciousness and apply it to your point of view. Be a broadcaster—on the top-side.

Today you are in the vibration of Universal Love and the Brotherhood of Man. You belong to the world at large and see everything in broad sweeps. You realize that you can do nothing for yourself alone, for 9 is a curved boomerang. Since the number stands at the top of the Cycle, it gets a bird's-eye view of the Universe and has no conception of pettiness or detail,—only a vision of the ultimate goal. You can sense that it has included you in the vibration of all the truly great who have ever lived—artists, philanthropists, altruists; you are one with them and share their thoughts and motives. Today you cannot become impatient with opposition or despise another's point of view, for you realize that you were once, a very short time ago, as unenlightened as those others who are looking through the wrong end of the telescope. You are so thrilled with the new outlook that you want to give everyone a hand-up and let all share it. You realize that tomorrow will start a new cycle of achievement and are, therefore, determined to leave no loose ends to be carried over; if you do, they will drag along interminably. You are closing a chapter and are wise enough to do it effectively and thoroughly. Mistakes and ugliness are all beneath and behind you.

"God's in His heaven; all's right with the world."

TAKE THE INVENTORY.

An 11-Day

REVELATION

Forget business, as business, and the pursuit of money. Slow down on active work. Give yourself time to look for the vision ahead and get a focus on the revelation. Express your ideals. Show to everyone you meet the beauty of the thing at hand. Know your own strength and weakness. Force no issues. Keep at peace. Deal with the public—not to exploit yourself, but to give out your knowledge. Spend some time in the clouds, but don't become a nuisance by missing appointments. Don't worry about commercializing anything—improve it first. Be a comfort, if anyone seems to need or want it. Keep the sun shining inside of you. Put aside the hard-boiled practicalities for another day; be a dreamer, visionary, idealist, *revealer* of the things that others may not have noticed. Don't reduce yourself to 2.

Today may mean for you a big step forward or it may throw you—according to the way in which you handle it. It is not easy, for it has little to do with practical affairs. It stands for a new beginning in a higher Cycle, or a deeper sinking in an old rut. It bears a close resemblance to 7 in some of its qualities, but differs from it inasmuch as it is not yours. It offers new visions of Utopian fields, opens doors to new attainments, brings inspiration for greater achievement—to be handed on to others! It is a bridge to the gods —shown to you in order that you may show it to others. It is the Light of the World—*for* the world. It brings no personal rewards except through service and healing. It exacts faith, reverence, worship. It demands the expression of your best. It "shows you up" as you are. It is one of the two Master Numbers.

FOLLOW THE STAR.

A 22-DAY

THE MATERIAL MASTER

Work your ideals. Bring order and system into the eternal truths you know. Explain them in words of one syllable and give everyone a chance to *use* them. Burst into song, but see that it becomes a Community affair. Devise a practical solution of all the burdens that are brought to you. Make big plans, but be sure they are possible of accomplishment. Organize something that has great scope for general improvement. Put your vision into working form.

This is the day when earth and heaven meet. Even the sky is not the limit, for your visionary power goes beyond. You can build, today, a solid, practical foundation for the air-castle of your 11-day. You are adding to your practical, working 4 all the vision and imagination of your 11—twice over. You are using your powerful, successful 5, your artistic, expressive 3, your stabilizing 6, your spiritual 7, your universal 9—all moulded together into a master-building. You are the Race Messenger.

THE MASTER VIBRATES 22.

SPECIAL DAYS FOR EVERYBODY

1-2-3.....Best for shopping—for clothes, adornments, art objects.

5 ....Best for buying on margin or other speculation. Also for advertising or selling or promoting.

6 ....Best for buying for the home—all supplies, household commodities or decorations. Best for moving into a new home.

7 ....Best for Savings' Bank deposits.

1-2-4-8-22 Best for making deposits in checking accounts.

9.........Best for making public appearances or gifts.

> Don't try to *finish* on a 1; START.
> Don't try to *start* on a 9; FINISH.
> Don't buy tickets for travelling on a 2, 4 or 6.
> Don't stay home on a 5.
> Don't travel on a 6.
> Don't start anything you can't finish on a 6.
> Don't do *anything* on a 7 except analyze and perfect.

Don't be afraid to do any *necessary* thing on *any* day; first tune in your attitude of mind according to the number of the day—then go ahead.

PART II

FOR THOSE WHO WANT TO KNOW MORE

CHAPTER I

SYMBOLISM

SYMBOLISM is as old as the human race and the first record of man's attempt to understand his relationship to his Creator.

There are many types of symbols, increasing in intricacy and hidden meaning as the wise of all ages have pursued their quest for Truth, but the basic Pythagorean axiom "God geometrizes" gives us the clue to the simplest and most universal form and shows us the inevitable numerological foundation upon which all Beginnings rest.

In considering the "Cause behind all Causes" or the fundamental Principle behind all creation we are attempting to set a limitation to the Limitless and to define the Unimaginable. We must, therefore, apply a boundary in order to reduce the subject to the limits of our understanding.

Before *anything* we must think of the unmanifested *everything* which to our minds must appear as a Force existent in Eternity, endowed with omnipotence. Since we must enclose it in order to conceive of it, we may symbolize it, as did the Ancients, by a Circle—a figure without beginning and without end. Since we know that God *is* and that we *are,* we must next imagine this Force as once containing within Itself an urge or impulse for creation and for that purpose retiring to a center, which we may represent by a dot within the Circle. The dot, by extension or elongation of itself becomes the

1. THE INITIAL FLAME—UNITY

Thus have we defined the upright geometrical line. In this 1 is all *potential* creative force—the first radiation—but it is still a *single* Principle and if it is to go forward, another Principle must be added or it remains forever 1. The next step, then is division or setting a part of Itself beside Itself, thus becoming

2. DUALITY

Here are the positive and negative poles, the Male-Female Principle, the separateness in fusion—the Father-Mother.

$$\bigwedge$$

From this fusion results a third element—the Son—giving us, as a result

3. EXPRESSION—TRINITY

To the united 1 and 1 we add a base-line and form the triangle—the Eternal Trinity of Father-Mother-Son, the Expression of Creation.

$$\triangle$$

From Expression followed the next step—Form—and this we find in

4. BOUNDARY

This is the first manifestation in matter—MAN—the opening of the Triangle to form the Square

▢

of Spirit (1), Soul (2), Mind (3) and Body (4). Within the enclosure of the square Man begins his first lessons. He learns to till his field, to struggle with the four elements, to lay his own foundation and build his own building. That accomplished, he is no longer content with the protection of the square, but begins to sense its limitation. He has awakened to *awareness* in

5. EXPANSION

He erases one of the sides of the square and begins to seek to discover what lies outside.

⌂

He is becoming alive to the repetition, in himself, of the 5 symbols from which he sprang—the circle, the dot, the line, the triangle and the square; he finds their number in his five senses, five fingers and five toes—in the form of his arms, legs and torso, in the original five planets and five vowels. He begins his wanderings in the joy of freedom—and ends them in loneliness. He feels his own incompleteness and through his awareness of the Origin of himself, strives for emulation in seeking another to set beside himself. This he finds in

6. UNION; HARMONIZATION

The Fire Triangle—"As above" finds its reflection in the Water Triangle—"So Below"

Man has completed himself in his "polar opposite" and has himself become the creator. For the security of his expression he returns to the basic *form* of his original square and builds upon the cube.

His own image is extended in his children, his work carried on by them; his creative urge is satisfied, his material task completed. He has been *aware* of the reflection, within himself, of the "First Cause," but he has never paused to consider his definite relationship. To discover the "link between" he turns within to examine his own Soul. Through this examination and analysis he discovers the principle of

7. PERFECTION

From the square of himself and the Basic Trinity behind it (the 4 and the 3) he learns the completion and perfection of the great cosmic number 7 and marks its recurrence in the 7 days, 7 colors, 7 notes of the scale, 7 planets. He takes his first Initiation and withdraws from the world of action. He finds that 7 is not the number of the Cycle of Man and that his own material tasks are not yet completed.

To these he must return in

8. MANIFESTATION

From the stronghold of his period of meditation and reflection he has gathered the necessary power to master the forces of matter and the balanced judgment to use them for the good of his fellow man. In 8 he completes his own octave. He builds again upon the square—but now he understands the extension of all its angles—the square upon the square.

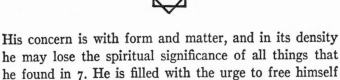

His concern is with form and matter, and in its density he may lose the spiritual significance of all things that he found in 7. He is filled with the urge to free himself from material concern and through this urge finds

9. UNIVERSAL LOVE

Only through the Father-Mother-Son principle can his power reach the whole world. The Triangle is *squared* to

material need and he himself a "spectator," viewing the
two material squares—God's and man's—from above.

He has now completed his own Cycle. He began with the
o (God) behind the 1; progressed to the state of awareness in 5 (the number of man); took his spiritual initiation in 7 (the Cosmic Number); returned to material
manifestation in 8 (the first *free* number) and finished
his task of Universal Service in 9.

In 10 he returns to bring all things back to the Source
—this time with the vision (o) *ahead* of his beginning
(1). Return to Unity.

In 11 a new beginning is made in a higher Cycle. He is
a messenger of God and a Master among men. His task
is Revelation.

What he sees in 11 and reveals to his fellow men he is
not always able to put into concrete form, so he goes on
until he finds complete material dominion and Mastery in
22—the sum of the Trinity (3), the Planets (7), the
Signs of the Zodiac (12)—the 22 symbols of the Hebrew
alphabet, picturing the summation of Wisdom and Creation in the 22 Tarot Cards.

CHAPTER II

ALPHABETS

"WORDS are sound; Sound the result of vibration; Vibration the source of Form."

Sound is the result of vibration—which is only another way of saying that every sound has a *number* behind it. Each letter of every alphabet has its distinctive sound (or how else could we distinguish between them?) and therefore, its distinctive number.

The connection between letter and number was first discovered by students of the Arabic and it was in Arabia that the system of *reduction* of numbers was first used—called "Jaffar." This system of "final digitting" was brought to the Hebrews by Moses and to the Greeks by Pythagoras and is used today in Numerology as invaluable in determining the *Essence* of what lies behind.

In Chaldean the same signs identically are used for both numbers and letters. In Hebrew every letter has its number, and words having the same numerical value have an invariable correspondence in meaning.

Every race responds to and is influenced by its *own* alphabet, and by their own alphabets should their names be "Charted." An oriental, born and brought up in the East responds to the vibrations of his own letter-sounds and only when he leaves his own country, assumes a different name and *vibrates* to the new environment can his numbers be determined by the alphabet-values of the adopted land. A Hebrew, living in a country where the Hebrew Number-Kabbala is used, should be charted by that alphabet; a Greek by his own; we of the West by ours.

Every alphabet in every tongue has its own undeviating sequence, established by custom or necessity, and the *meaning* of a letter is mirrored in the shape the letter takes.

In our own alphabet we use our letter-values according to their numerical sequence—although there are some systems of Numerology that assign a value of 9 to *each* letter, no matter what its position in the alphabet. This has been found to be faulty and inaccurate. 9 is the number of the microcosmic Cycle of Man, but it is *not* the number of each one of his experiences as they are revealed in the letter-"transits" of his name. The *duration* of these experiences varies according to the numerical position of each letter, for there is a *law* which determines their sequence in the alphabet and by this law is their number *fixed*.

There is also a law which governs the *form* of each letter. Forms vary according to meanings. Our letter D, as 4, is *enclosed*, for 4 means to us a field with prescribed boundaries. The Cretan, Phoenician and Greek symbols for D (Daleth, Delta) Δ are also closed. The Hebrew D (Daleth) ד is open, for to the Hebrews D is a door and not an enclosure.

Many interesting correspondences and differences may be found by studying alphabets, but the final truth to be realized is that there is a *reason* behind every form—and that that reason is found in the rate of vibration.

Number itself, in the last analysis, reverts to the same fundamental meaning in all tongues and for all countries; alphabets are individual and localized.

Work out your own name by your own alphabet—the one you use and live with every day; it is YOURS and will tell you the truth about yourself.

CHAPTER III

FURTHER ASPECTS OF YOUR NAME

The Inclusion

In Part 1 we considered the name-vibration from the aspects of Soul Urge, Quiescent Self and Expression.

To learn the whole story of yourself it is necessary to look beyond the revelations of the final digits and consider in detail the meaning of *each letter* as a "tool" given you to carve your way through life. For this purpose it is necessary to set up a more complicated Chart than we did when we were concerned mainly with the final numbers and the digits of the separate names. You will find it convenient to use the symbols for Soul Urge, Quiescent Self and Expression in common use in Numerology and such others as are here suggested or that you may devise yourself.

The symbol for the Soul Urge is the Circle— ◯

"   "   for the Quiescent Self is the Square— ▢

"   "   for the Expression is the Triangle— △

As an example we will set up the name of GEORGE WASHINGTON

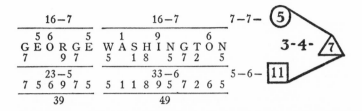

It is not sufficient to find the Soul Urge and Quiescent Self (sum of the vowels and sum of the consonants) and add them together. *Always* take a further step and another line and set *all* the number values in a row under their respective letters. Only in this way can you learn what is actually behind the Expression.

For example, a 6 Soul Urge with a 5 Quiescent Self do not always give a true 11 Expression; and, by the same token, we might lose sight of an 11 or 22 in the Expression by omitting the longer process.

Be very careful about assigning 11's and 22's indiscriminately. To few are given these great vibrations, for few are Masters. *Never* add together two of three names or two of three Cycles to produce a Master Number; that is "juggling" and is not a true result. Work only for "true" finals, but never lose sight of the Master Numbers if they appear as *one* of the results behind the final. For the purposes of *addition* they may be reduced; for the purposes of *consideration* they are left intact.

We now have all the letters with their number values that are *included* in the name of GEORGE WASHINGTON. We will first consider the numbers and see how many he has of each. This will show us what points were *intensified* in his nature; to what degree he was well-balanced or ill-balanced—of what he had much or little;

and in what respects, if any, he was lacking. We then proceed to set up the

TABLE OF THE INCLUSION

We have only to examine the name and note the numbers on the last line, selecting them in their order and setting them down in a column.

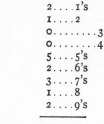

```
2 .... 1's
1 .... 2
0 ........ 3
0 ........ 4
5 ... 5's
2 .... 6's
3 ... 7's
1 .... 8
2 .... 9's
```

Total 16

We now have a much more accurate "line" on George Washington than we had from a knowledge of his Soul Urge and Expression and much more information as to his general characteristics and minor traits.

We find that, through the two 1's he had the qualities of pioneer, leader and independent creator; that he had courage and persistence and enough will power to see his plans through to completion. There are but *two* 1's in the Table, so we need not conclude that he was over-insistent in leadership or over-ambitious for self alone.

The 2 enabled him to work with others and defer to their opinions, exercise any necessary tact and diplomacy and be sensitive to the feelings and preferences of those with whom he was associated.

We find that he is lacking in 3 and 4. Through the lack of 3 he would find some difficulty with the easy flow of words and would be obliged to make a conscious effort to overcome it. He would not be tempted, however, to scatter his forces uselessly and while he might not always be alive to the lighter side of beauty and the joy of living, nor given to seeking an audience for the exploitation of his own talents, he would not be called upon to make a constant *effort* toward stabilization.

Through the lack of 4 he would often be confronted with the necessity for patience and the need of working slowly and carefully. He would also, in his private life, incline toward unconventionality and refuse to be a slave to custom or tradition. He would have to learn order and system and could not always yield to his desire to leave all details to others.

The 5 seems somewhat overbalanced in comparison with the rest of the numbers. We must remember, however, that 5 is the "Number of Man" and that he who is lacking in the vibration has much to learn in the school of experience before he can attain to any understanding of life or his fellow man. 5 gives the qualities of versatility, adaptability, urge for progress and expansion and the passion for freedom that brings release from all limitation. *Many* 5's incline to too much freedom, especially along the lines of the five senses, but 5, being free, can go up as well as down, so we must form no fixed conclusions until we know from which of the three aspects any number has been handled.

The two 6's gave him a keen sense of responsibility and a willingness to bear burdens and make adjustments for those looking to him for help and leadership. It is the number of the Cosmic Father (or Mother) as well as that of the more domestic parent.

The three 7's gave tremendous force to his powers of mental analysis and ability to search for hidden truths and causes. He indeed examined the *fundamentals* before he acted and *perfected* every plan before it was launched.

The 8 gave him mastery over material forces and conditions, balanced judgment and the right use of the power that made him materially free.

The force of 9 is not over-strong, showing that his concern was more with his own community and country than with world affairs. Fortunate for us that it was, for he came into leadership at a time when all his forces were needed at home. He was very universal in his impulses, however, for he gave all emoluments to charity and was ever alive to the need for general improvement and for bettering the conditions of the people.

The "7" was further expressed in his later days when he retired from public life, sought the country that he loved and found peace in his own garden.

The Ruling Passion

Although we may go far in this type of analysis, we must form no final judgments, for there are many points not yet touched upon, all of which must be related to the three main numbers. One of these points is the "Ruling Passion." This may be—and usually is—quite different from the Soul Urge for it indicates the pet fad or hobby that may have no concern with "development" or "progress" and is not so much HOW you do things as WHAT you most *enjoy* doing. Always remembering that 5, being the "natural" number, must not be counted too literally, else it would dominate the majority of Tables—a safe rule to follow, when calculating the Ruling Passion, is to subtract 2 from the number of 5's in the list and *then* see which number appears in greatest proportion; 5 may still be the Ruling Passion, or it may divide the honors with another number, but make an allowance of 2 in the case of 5, before you begin to figure.

In the case of George Washington, after subtracting 2 from his number of 5's, we see that 5 and 7 are equal in force, so we would give him *two* Ruling Passions, one of Freedom (5) and the other of Mental Analysis (7).

JUDGING THE INCLUSION TABLE

A few general rules may be followed in regard to the Inclusion Table:—

Many 1's show strong opinions and domination—probably egotism; much courage, independence and vital energy.

Few 1's (or none) show that the Self is not of first importance.

The individual, however, may lack ambition and initiative.

Many 2's show fine consideration for others, romanticism, sensitivity, grace, rhythm, friendliness, cooperation, detail and emotionalism.

Few 2's (or none) show lack of adaptability, carelessness in detail, unwillingness to cooperate, lack of consideration for others.

Many 3's show inspiration, imagination, lightheartedness, gift of expression—WORDS, extravagance, impatience, scattering.

Few 3's show limited emotional expression,

difficulty with flow of language, absence of showmanship, inferiority complex.

Many 4's show concentration, sense of values, love of form, willingness to work; often stubbornness and narrow-mindedness.

Few 4's (or none) show aversion to labor (laziness), order and system; impatience, dislike of routine.

Many 5's show love of change, social possibilities, opportunity for publicity, nervousness, haste, impulsiveness, love of pleasure and the world, interest in all things, resourcefulness, tendency to tear down and run away to the new.

Few 5's show dislike of crowds, lack of constructive curiosity, inability to "discard," little understanding, limited life-experience.

Many 6's show willingness to assume responsibility, power of adjustment and harmonization. (If there are more than two 6's, the individual is likely to be given *cosmic* responsibilities.) May be stubborn and ingrained, with unyielding ideals and self-righteousness.

Few 6's (or none) show dislike of responsibility and neglect of duty.

Many 7's (rare) show technique, analysis, questioning, research, love of *facts,* mental keenness. (7, in strong force, if not constructively handled, gives a tendency to drink, scheming and secretiveness.)

Few (none) show acceptance of surface appearances, refusal to reason, lack of spiritual awareness.

Many 8's show over-anxiety for attainment, ability to succeed and make things pay, executive ability, money-consciousness.

Few (none) show the individual is not a born financier; carelessness or disregard of material values, inability to manage affairs.

Many 9's show generosity and impressionability, emotionalism, humanitarianism, artistic and oratorical ability.

Few show little concern with service or humanity, interest centered in friends or community, narrow outlook, no understanding of the emotional reactions of others.

(Note: See if one of the listed 2's is K (11) or one of the 4's V (22). These must not be judged as 2 and 4).

We will go on to a further analysis of this Table and see what else it has to reveal about the individual.

CHAPTER IV

THE KARMIC LESSONS

IT was with a purpose that we extended the missing numbers beyond the line in the Inclusion Table, for they "stick out like sore thumbs" in our life and cannot be made too prominent in our consideration.

The missing numbers in the name indicate experiences consciously and deliberately evaded and avoided in the past. The ultimate aim of Perfected Man is to include *all* the vibrations in *balanced* quantity—but when that is finally attained the obligation for reincarnation no longer exists and we are unbound from the "Wheel of Necessity." We may, however, *strive* for this equilibrium and we *must*, whether we will or no, "make up" *now*, in the present life-experience, the lessons of the past that we have refused to learn.

Never having contacted them, we are ignorant of them —and because we are ignorant of them, we fear them. It may be true to say "What we don't know doesn't worry us" but what we don't know *about* does worry us when we are obliged to meet it. The missing numbers must be pushed back into the Table and included in our Subconscious, along with the others we already have and are using. They are the weak links in the character and must be strengthened. Learn we must, but there are two ways of learning—Because of and In Spite of. Life always takes a hand in teaching us; if we accept the lessons and profit by them *because* we realize their necessity and *want* to, we learn the lessons more easily and less painfully; if we use resistance, Life takes charge of the entire job and *forces* upon us experiences—in the form of knocks and hardships—that make us fully conscious of the meaning of the things we lack. This is Karma—the fulfilment of the Law, the inevitable Effect of Cause—*In spite* of ourselves.

If the missing number or numbers appear elsewhere—as in Soul Urge or Expression—it has less of the quality of Karma, but still represents a weak link that must now be attacked with especial intensity. The one having many Karmic Lessons has added difficulty in life until the lessons are learned—the numbers "made up"—for until that time arrives, he cannot give his full attention to the Life Path, nor is he free to embrace its opportunities—he is too busy getting to his feet after being repeatedly knocked down. Those who have attained to that stage of development which make them *seek* a knowledge of their relationship with life are in a fair way to overcome their Karma rapidly; those who choose to remain in the "victim" class will be given every opportunity to do so. The weakest spot is the one that is always assailed the hardest: as soon as it becomes strengthened, the strain is no longer felt—and there is always a definite compensation to be had from fulfilled Karma. There is sometimes found a subconscious urge to supply the missing numbers, which often results in an overdoing of the lesson and consequent negativity or unbalance. Equilibrium is the Great Law.

We have only to remember that Karma is a phase of experience that meets us at every turn; that we do not like it because we do not know it; that we fear it because we are ignorant of the advantages it may bring us; that if we wait for Life to teach us about it, we shall first become acquainted with its more difficult side, and that if we accept it willingly and consciously, we may benefit by it in every experience we contact.

TABLE OF THE KARMIC LESSONS

1

Evidence of self-effacement in the past—an unwillingness to meet issues squarely; lack of trust in the inherent power; lack of initiative; difficulty in making decisions; dread of being the first in the field; unwillingness to seek interviews or promote the self; over-caution; fear; dread of making a beginning. He starts after many delays—often too late—and only from pressure.

Life will force him into situations where he must make his own decisions. Whenever he contacts the vibration of 1, in Cycle, Pinnacle, Year, Month or Day the need to strengthen his own individuality will be brought home to him. He will have to *fight* for his own place. Children born in January or October, if "Minus 1," should never be repressed and should be trained to rely upon themselves and make their own decisions. They should be encouraged to leave home at an early age.

2

The importance of detail, patience, tact and obedience has been overlooked. There is a tendency to neglect small things or gloss over them, to disregard time and appointments and to fail to *collect* and *accumulate* the small things.

Life will force him into situations where he can achieve nothing without great patience and attention to detail. Details will press upon him and exclude the aim in view because of the infinite number of small steps to climb and little weeds to pull up. He will be shy, yet obliged to mix with others; he will find that tact, diplomacy and friendliness are the necessary things to accomplish his purpose. He will prefer to work alone and find himself in need of help. The presence of 11 will, in some measure, compensate for this lack—but not altogether. 11 is a higher vibration and more concerned with theories and ideals. Kleptomaniacs are usually found to be "Minus 2"; the urge to make up the Karma produces a desire for collection. Without the urge, everything slips through the fingers and nothing is saved.

3

This is an avoidance of self-expression—often indicated by faulty posture. Minus 3 will often be round-shouldered, through a desire to enclose himself and seek protection from the gaze of the world. There has been a lack of self-esteem and self-confidence—no desire to promote the personality. There is a psychological slump in the mind which is often conveyed to the body.

Life will force him into situations where he will be in need of the dramatic and expressional quality. Lacking the ability to advertise and sell, he will be obliged to do both. He will constantly under-sell himself and wear an apologetic air—which will invariably defeat him.

4

This indicates a former resentment of the slow, material vibration of 4. Hard work, as such, has been avoided and former experiences of ease, luxury and money have made this possible. There is a fear that labor means only hardship and limitation. There is a strong tendency to take short cuts and avoid effort.

Life will show him that he can accomplish nothing without starting at the foundation and *working* carefully and slowly. He will be made to see that every sacrifice of patience and foundation to *speed* results in eventual crash.

5

This is the indication of having dodged not only human relationships but life experiences. There is poor equipment with which to go through life—no understanding or toleration, no versatility or adaptability—only the constant fear of the new and progressive. This is a rare lack for, being the "number of man" experiences have been necessary. The Minus 5 has refused to profit by them, walking through them with closed eyes.

Life will place him in situations where a knowledge of the world is essential; where he will meet with constant change and be obliged to face many emergencies. He will be made to realize that some phase of development may be gained from every experience and life will be a tragedy until he learns something about his fellow man.

6

Responsibility has been avoided or refused. There has been an aversion to being tied down and a fear of taking on any obligations. Many things have been undertaken but nothing *finished;* the value and beauty of service is unknown; associations have been avoided and only the self emphasized.

Life will show the Minus 6 that friends and family will do little or nothing for him but rather, will require much from him; he will be burdened with their care and support—often in an unwelcome or disagreeable way—and will have many adjustments to make in his own life and those of others. He will be loaded with responsibilities and be given the opportunity to discharge all obligations; he will have thrust upon him the more difficult lessons of domesticity. Minus 6 has much to learn about being a good wife or husband— because he is ignorant of the necessary adjustments of this relationship. If married, failure to learn this lesson usually leads to separation or divorce. A Minus 6 child should be given pets and responsibilities. A Minus 6 adult may nullify the Karma by adopting a child—but it may be hard on the child.

7

This shows an unwillingness to train the mind along scientific lines, to examine causes before reaching conclusions or accepting results. It is also an indication of neglect of the inner or spiritual life. The lack of 7 in the majority of adult Tables today is the result of the dualism preached throughout the Piscean Age. Spirituality meant to the majority isolation, penance, fasting and prayer, hair shirts and flagellation; the "spiritual" class of people were apart—monks, nuns, hermits—and what they represented had no place in everyday life and no connection with any of its pleasanter things. Thus did *fear* attach itself to 7.

Life will continually give the opportunity to replace the fear with faith—through bereavement, poverty, loneliness and isolation. The Minus 7 will be thrown upon his own resources—turned *in* upon himself—and forced to distinguish between the transitory and the permanent—the material and the spiritual.

8

Things material and physical have been avoided. Financial cowardice and the fear of taking chances; doubt of the ability to handle material situations; lack of efficiency in business; carelessness or strain in money matters. Poor judgment.

Life will insist upon his handling his own affairs. He will suddenly acquire a sum of money, immediately scatter it and then be made to keenly feel its lack. The Minus 8 will find his hands tied until he learns the wise distribution of his own funds; if he is without money he will strain after its attainment; if he uses his millions wholly for self-promotion or indulgence, he will be made to feel the *burden* of it—being deprived of health, happiness or satisfaction in the gratification of his desires. Karma works either as lack or *misuse*—and always insists upon an understanding of the LAW.

9

This is rare and unfortunate. Every other experience has been contacted except that of learning the human angle. There has been a fear of the emotions and no understanding of them in others. There is no appreciation of suffering, for the *fire* of life has been missed. The concern has been centered upon the self and the law of past lives has been not to get involved or concerned with anything that lay outside.

Life will offer jolt after jolt to the emotional nature until it is thoroughly awakened. The minus 9 will be called upon to relinquish all without personal satisfaction or reward. He will go through the fire of intense emotional suffering until he acquires love, sympathy and understanding of the sufferings of those who live on the emotional plane. He will have to acquire what he formerly lacked— red blood.

The numbers most frequently missing are 7 and 8; 4 and 2 next; then 6, 3 and 1.

5 and 9 are usually found.

CHAPTER V

THE SUBCONSCIOUS SELF

THIS is a sort of emanation or "aura" that the individual carries about with him and *is*—often more evident to his friends than to himself. It is, therefore, the "unselfconscious self" and represents the total of the various *kinds* of vibration that are actually in the Inclusion. It is no indication of ability; it gives no conscious urge or impulse; it is simply What You Are as a human being and how you react to human relationships and situations. It is not to be confused with the Quiescent Self, for while they are both, in a sense, "latent," the Quiescent Self is not concerned with relationships or reactions and the Subconscious Self is wholly concerned with both. They do work together, however, and many interesting comparisons may be made between them.

The Subconscious Self is emotional rather than mental and shows your *response* in moments of crisis or emergency—when there has been no time to refer the situation to the brain.

In discovering the nature of this vibration we again consult the Inclusion Table to learn *what* vibrations it contains and *what* it lacks. Here we are not concerned with the quantity or number of *each* one, but simply— "Have I the 1-vibration, the 7," etc. Since 9 represents the highest total to be found in the Inclusion, whatever is lacking from this total (i.e. the Karmic Lessons) must be subtracted from 9 in order to learn what you actually have to work with.

For example, if there are two Karmic Lessons, 2 must be subtracted from 9—in that case the Subconscious will be 7; if there are three Karmic Lessons, 3 must be subtracted from 9—leaving 6 as the Subconscious number. It naturally follows that, the greater the number of Karmic Lessons, the lower will be the number of the Subconscious.

3 is the lowest Subconscious Number that is found— and that rarely, for it implies *six* Karmic Lessons and seldom is an individual given such a burden to carry.

(An example of a Subconscious 3 is Jesse James, the noted bandit of the last century.)

TABLE OF THE SUBCONSCIOUS

3

This implies 6 Karmic Lessons. Here the individual would be utterly scattered and de-centralized. With only three types of things to work with, only three things of which he had had a former experience, the tendency would be to *fight* for their expression and he would meet constant opposition in the Karma. This would almost inevitably result in destructive reactions. 3 insists upon expression and, under resistance, explodes.

4

This implies 5 Karmic Lessons. The individual would be lost in the detail of everything he undertook. Hard and unceasing work would absorb his life and he would only,

with the greatest difficulty, attain to any success. His only
salvation would be concentration on *some* of his lacks,
coupled with a good specialized education; better still,
a change of name that would supply some of the vibrations with which he had to make acquaintance. In the
present case he would never be able to "see the woods
for the trees," could scarcely afford the time to sit down
to eat and would be so burdened with detail and slow
movement that he would never be able to take a step
ahead.

5

This implies 4 Karmic Lessons. This individual would be
very scattered and nervous, restless and dissatisfied. The
reactions would be trivial and inconsequential; in case of
fire he would seek all doors at once—and find none—or
run about in circles, screaming. He would be irresponsi-
ble, unconcentrated, chattering, pleasure-seeking, constantly demanding change. His viewpoint would be wholly
physical and material.

6

This implies 3 Karmic Lessons. This individual would
emanate comfort, love and concern for the welfare of all
in the vicinity. Home would be the center of the work
and the affections; the well-being of those nearest and
dearest would be the first consideration. In case of acci-
dent or crisis, the progress of all would be impeded by
the "6" gathering to his arms all the family, friends and
possessions and trying to stagger out with them.

7

This implies 2 Karmic Lessons. This individual is pre-occupied, aloof, sensitive, unobtrusive—often indifferent to what is going on around him. He is mental, analytical, well-balanced. He is a well of secrecy. He inwardly responds to love but outwardly throws cold water on it. If 7 is one of the Karmic Lessons, he will enjoy learning it—especially after 30 years of age; *or* if his 7 Subconscious belongs to a negative nature and the 7 is Karmic, he will probably take to drink. His reaction in crisis will be prayer.

8

This implies 1 Karmic Lesson. This individual will have a commercial attitude toward life and will handle unexpected situations efficiently, referring all things to reason. He will want to sell whatever he makes and will consider it a fault not to make everything pay. He is rather cold and matter of fact, but dependable and solid. He is strong for organization and, in a crisis, will know just what to do to extricate himself and others; he would immediately set everybody to work.

9

This implies no Karmic Lessons. Having done everything at least once, this individual is rather bored with life. He has a tendency to generalize and bring the *whole* to every part. He is too impersonal to be greatly concerned. He backs down quickly in an argument and can be "bluffed" out of his own opinion. He has a critical viewpoint, is interested *slightly* in everything, but violently in nothing. In a crisis, he is philosophical and resigned.

A convenient symbol for the Subconscious is $\wedge\!\!\!=$. As an example of its use we will repeat the Inclusion Table of George Washington.

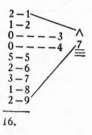

$$\begin{array}{l} 2-1 \\ 1-2 \\ 0----3 \\ 0----4 \\ 5-5 \\ 2-6 \\ 3-7 \\ 1-8 \\ 2-9 \end{array}$$

16.

CHAPTER VI

THE PLANES OF EXPRESSION

THERE are four planes, or fields of activity, on which we express ourselves—the Mental, the Physical, the Emotional and the Intuitional. Since through our given names we learn about our general equipment for life, by an examination of their separate vibrations we may discover our place of greatest power—the *plane* to which we bring the most knowledge and experience. This is valuable information when determining Vocation or considering our own fitness for a special type of work. Here we may learn whether we are better equipped for a business career, an artistic, a scientific, a literary or a diplomatic. This will help us to decide whether we shall go in for public life, writing, salesmanship, research, the drama, medicine, teaching, reforming or occultism. It will show us whether we are practical or "flighty," stable or over-emotional, inspired or material. This does not, however, give us the "last word" about Vocation; there are many factors to be taken into consideration—chief of which is the Life Path or Opportunity. It does show us the qualities we bring to our activities and gives us a general idea of our assets and liabilities.

There are, for example, many varieties of writers—scientific, religious, dramatic, critical, philosophical and fictional. There are many types of business men—artistic, commercial, those of large vision and the small shop-keeper. There are many types of artist—inspired, commercial, good and bad. There are many people totally unfitted for any kind of productive activity because of excess of emotionalism or mental unbalance. All of these are indicated by the Planes of Expression.

The rough division of "The Great Within" and "The Great Without" is too general to be depended upon. The consideration of mere *numbers* in the Inclusion Table is misleading and inaccurate. *Each letter* of the name must be considered and given its true position on the Planes.

Each Plane has three subdivisions—Inspired, Dual and Balanced; each letter has a place of its own—first on the plane to which it belongs; then in its own subdivision. There is no overlapping (as in the case of Numbers) no error in classification, for every letter in the alphabet has a history behind it.

TABLE OF THE PLANES OF EXPRESSION

	MENTAL	PHYSICAL	EMOTIONAL	INTUITIONAL
Inspired	A	E	O R I Z	K
Dual	H J N P	W	B S T X	F Q U Y
Balanced	G L	D M		C V

Those who have a preponderance of letters on the Mental Plane are equipped with the qualities necessary for business on a large scale, for writing on serious or technical subjects, for dealing in international concerns, for invention and for various types of rulership.

Those strong on the Physical Plane are more concerned with form and material manifestation than with the type of work that demands mentality. They have much human interest and concern for progress in material ways, are thoroughly practical and use their energies for tangible results.

The emotional people are artistic and *heart*istic, caring little for facts or analysis. They are creative, but are apt to run away with their own ideas. (It will be noted that there are no *balanced* letters on the Emotional Plane.)

Those whose greatest power is on the Intuitional Plane are absorbed in the Unseen and in the reception of spiritual facts. They are not practical except when well balanced (as in C and V)—and then only when they consciously detach themselves from the dream-world in which they usually live. They are inspired along inventive lines (as in K). The dual letters on this Plane give them adaptable qualities but do not help to stabilize them.

From the above Table will be seen the folly of generalizations and hasty conclusions when we are attempting to make a thorough analysis of the character or abilities. For example, A, J and S all have the value of 1 (see Table, Part 1, page 16). They all have qualities of leadership, originality, self-development and promotion—but they have important psychological differences that are especially evident in their transits (see Part 2, page 231). A and J are both mental, but A is inspired and *direct* and will go straight to its goal without deviation; J is also endowed with fine mentality and has the same qualities of leadership, but J does not always see things through to completion because it is inclined to vacillation through its ability to see all sides of a question. The inspired letters are the creators or *starters*, the dual letters *carry on* the process already begun and not until we reach the *balanced* vibrations may we be sure of constructive *termination*. S is thoroughly emotional; one may be sure of encountering an emotional upheaval during the transit of S; the mind is incapable of clear thought because the feelings are too much involved; the duality of the letter runs the gamut of emotional experience; the value of the letter ($19 = 1$) relates every event to the Self.

B, K and T, as 2 have differences as vital. B and T are both Emotional-dual; B retires into itself—shrinking, shy, needing love and protection, with no outgoing desire for experience or contact; B is given to tears and sensitiveness, falls in love easily and frequently and *lives* in its emotions. T is more spiritually evolved, more nervously tense, more eager for enlightenment and more concerned with self-sacrifice; it carries a cross and is constantly strained in its physical and emotional self. K is pure, inspired intuition; it returns by an effort from the vivid reality of vision. It is open and receptive *above,* open and revealing *below.*

C, L and U are 3—but with what vital differences! C is the symbol of the crescent moon, *tipped* so that its contents flow freely to men; as 3 it is the expression of the Trinity, as Moon it is intuitive, being *balanced;* its power expresses freely, joyously and constructively: C is truly psychic, but the owner is usually unaware of this power. L is straight, angular and Mental-balanced; its expression, as 3, is slow, sure and *reasoned* and has not the care-free spontaneity of C. U is the least expressive of all the 3's—indeed, it is so softened, inverted and receptive that its powers are much more attracting than out-giving.

It attracts to itself peculiar experiences, suffers much through its duality and weakness and, unless lived very positively, experiences loss and unhappiness.

D and M are Physical-balanced, set firmly upon earth and highly beneficial for outside, practical affairs. D contains all the necessary elements for mundane efficiency; it is enclosed and self-contained (like B), but not as emotional and not as aware; it has little concern with the divine nature inherent in form and swings along in its own rhythm of jocular, earthy well-being. Like all solids, it *holds* heat, cold or whatever conditions it contacts and thus is long in being realized and long in releasing its vibration. M is a net into which things are caught and trapped. It is the most inexpressive of all the letters, because it is the valley between high mountains and knows boundary rather than extent of vision. It is thorough and practical, affirming and approving *its own,* repressed and inarticulate—often hard and unfeeling— bound to materiality and form. V is the Intuitional—balanced Master—the cleaving plow working the field of humanity—and afterwards sowing the seed; it is open and receptive to the messages of the higher planes, pointed and powerful on the earth-plane.

E, although Physical, is capable of great inspiration which it puts into practice in material matters; it is well fitted to interpret the experience it has gained in terms of truth; it is helpful and practical—receiving from above and below, expressing usually in scientific form. N is the mentalization of truth—imaginative and therefore wavering (dual) but referring all things to the mind, sometimes in clear lights, sometimes in shadow. W is physical-dual —another valley between high mountains; it contains within itself the expressional urge (through its value of 5), but being physical, is apt to confine its wanderings to the realms of the senses—to its own remorse and unhappiness. It is a difficult letter, for it looks toward higher things but can seldom climb its own steep sides to reach them.

F is the cross surmounted by the Moon of intuition; as 6 it is the burden-bearer, in its own duality and uncertainty it suffers, but through its intuitional power it is capable of gaining the necessary equilibrium. O is beautiful, inspired, protected; self-enclosed; it is concerned with its own powers, silently brooding within; it gives out little for it is inherently conservative (6) and wants its own inspirations to grow into full flower before expressing them; it draws life to itself and remains poised and secure. Only when it is self-seeking and egotistic is it bound to the dogmatic and theologic, saying the things people want to hear from motives of expediency. X is crucifixion —the most karmic and most difficult of all the 6's. Through its duality it is seldom master of its own fate; it may be high-minded or debased, but it finds itself called upon to make so many emotional adjustments that it is in a constant state of turmoil and upheaval; sacrifice is its daily portion.

G is the mental Soul. It needs understanding of values and realities to steer its 7 from the realms of the tragic: it is aloof and introspective, although balanced and rhythmical in its large, outgoing lobe of expression. P is also Mental, but lacking the determination and will power of G. It is usually self-sufficient, but inexpressive of its innermost feelings—first as 7, next because it is not always sure of them itself (duality). It may be of an agnostic or atheistical turn of mind, but may babble cleverly on the subjects of faith or dogma. Y is the fork in the road—the Two Ways. With uplifted arms it reaches out into the dim light ahead, but through its duality is uncertain of which way to choose; it has no great degree of efficiency but is gifted with fine powers of perception. It can be a most beautiful or a most evil and tragic letter.

H is a ladder or a bridge, from one plane of consciousness to another—a step up from the material to the mental; there is always the impetus for *advance,* but the vacillation of the mind induces strain in producing the necessary force. Q is possessed of a dangerous power, for it functions in two worlds and is subject to under- or over-balance from the flood of White Light which it is capable of receiving. It is closely connected with the Pineal Center and the uncertain guidance of its high power in 8. It is rare and difficult to carry, often producing peculiar personalities and uncertain habits. It may mean temporary insanity or great genius. Z has the power of uniting the heaven and earth planes through its gift of inspiration and its understanding of human emotions. It suffers through its own excesses but has a straight line of union from the heart to the spirit and on this line succeeds in bridging emotional crises.

I and R are Emotional-Inspired. I is a torch—the candle at the window of the soul—or lightning, straight, clear and deadly; it may guide the wanderer home or be the flash of the murderer's knife; heart and passion rule the mind. It is a beautiful and high-powered force, but is apt to be destructive in large quantities. R is more undulating and more beautiful. It is the most selfless and understanding of all the letters. It is only through its boundless acceptance and toleration of man's failings that it is sometimes considered evil, because it is imposed upon by less developed souls. It, too, has high vibratory power and causes strain on the organisms that are incapable of attaining its speed. When it is handled through its numerical value of 9, there will be no difficulty in coping with it.

These are the values of the letters on the Planes. They have additional indications when in transit and these will be discussed in the Chapter on the Immediate Period Table.

CHAPTER VII

THE FOUR ELEMENTS

IN every individual there is a certain proportion or combination of the four elements: Fire, Earth, Air, Water. In relation to the birthdate the calculation must be made largely from an astrological standpoint; in relation to the *name* the calculation is made according to the numerical value of the letters and also of the digits resulting from their sums.

The Trinities of the Four elements are as follows:—

FIRE—1, 3, 9.
EARTH—4, 6, 8.
AIR—5, 6, 11
WATER—2, 7, 22.

The union of the Fire and Water trinities is frequently seen in the "interlaced triangles" symbol of the number 6—thus:—

✡

Keeping to the symbology of the triangle for all the elements, they may be pictured as follows:—

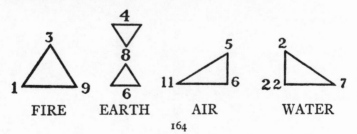

FIRE   EARTH   AIR   WATER

It will be noted that 6 is given both as Earth and Air. This is inherently true of the number; in its less evolved state 6 is concerned with material and personal love, physical comfort, external harmony and general well-being: when "stepped up" to its higher possibilities it is the peace and equilibrating force of air (which can also cause wind-storms of various descriptions) and the quiet, harmonious *sureness* of a love that extends beyond personal satisfaction. It is not the *fire* of love, despite its emotional qualities, for Fire is inherently tempestuous, less sure and often fatal for any continued love-relation.

> FIRE is Feeling
> Earth is Body
> Air is Spirit
> Water is Mind.

Earth is the negative pole of Fire; Water the negative pole of Air: Therefore, earth-qualities may be *transmuted* to fire-qualities and Fire may be said to "unlock" (release) Earth. By this are Body and material concern lifted to the realms of inspirational feeling.

Water-qualities may be transmuted to Air-qualities or be *unlocked* by Air. By this the Mind may be made to function in the realms of Spirit.

Fire can unlock Water only when, by contact, it rises as *steam* and represents the power which drives on to victory.

Air cannot unlock Earth, since heat is required to raise vibration.

Numbers of the same element cannot *unlock* each other, but may *help* each other by intensifying the power within them.

Air, sound and Water are co-related.

Light, Fire and Earth are co-related.

Each of the trinities contains three degrees; the first degree is concerned with Personal relationships, the second with Group and the third with Universal.

In the Fire Trinity—1-3-9—1 represents change, activity and energy related to the individual; 3 expresses light and beauty to the community; 9 uses love as a principle, universally.

In the Earth Trinity—4-6-8—4 is personal service, application and patient endurance; 6 gives love to its immediate relatives and friends and cares for their material wants; 8 uses its power in the world of form.

In the Air Trinity—5-6-11—5 is concerned with his own progress, versatility, freedom and understanding of life *as lived;* the love of 6 is stepped up to devotion and extends beyond its own circle; 11 lives in the spiritual atmosphere, there formulates its ideals and gives the revelation to the Universe.

In the Water Trinity—2-7-22—2 is peaceful, useful, beautiful, quiet, concerned with its own emotions and reactions; 7 is the fluid of the mental and spiritual planes—flowing between the two and making the passage of ideas, thoughts and accumulated *wisdom* valuable to those who come and seek it; 22 is Water of the most fundamental character, permeating all worlds and planes; the *form* which it produces is a by-product of the higher activity; thus does 22 become the Material Master.

Earth and Water need an education. Fire and Air succeed through inspiration. Fire mixes best with Air; Earth mixes best with Water; Air mixes with both.

THE ELEMENTS IN ASSOCIATION

FIRE

Fire with Fire— Too much force.
Fire with Earth— Disciplinary.
Fire with Air— Congenial.
Fire with Water— Powerful (as steam) or explosive.

EARTH

Earth with Fire— Disciplinary.
Earth with Earth— Slow and material.
Earth with Air— Unadaptable.
Earth with Water—Congenial.

AIR

Air with Fire— Congenial.
Air with Earth— Unadaptable.
Air with Air— Superficial and unstable.
Air with Water— Congenial.

WATER

Water with Fire— Powerful (as steam) or explosive.
Water with Earth— Congenial.
Water with Air— Congenial.
Water with Water— Static, unprogressive, introspective.

This information is very valuable when making a comparison of the numbers of your own Chart or those of one with whom you are contemplating association. It is also helpful when selecting a Vocation.

(See Chapter on Comparisons and Associations, page 223.)

CHAPTER VIII

CORNERSTONE, KEY NUMBER AND FIRST VOWEL

Your "Cornerstone" is the first letter of your first name. This is the *first* vibratory influence that contacts the new child and if the child has been named before birth, the influence will be felt as soon as the name is given, provided intra-uterine life has already begun. This letter has a vital "hook-up" with the birthdate, whose influence is around the child just preceding, during and after birth. This cornerstone is the thing upon which you are founded or built and, according to its nature and qualities, will have a restricting, stabilizing, vitalizing or debilitating effect upon your entire life. Its influence is more felt on the material plane than on the spiritual and does not give the *inner* urge (as does the Soul Number) but rather the natural inclination and viewpoint as related to material experience. It is one of the main considerations when contemplating a change of name, for it supports or inhibits the Expression.

The "Key Number" is the sum of the vibrations of the *first* name only. This is the next vibration that contacts the new child and even if the name has not yet been decided upon, it is latent in the parents' consciousness and therefore affecting the child. This is the weapon that unlocks (or fails to) each experience as it is met, each letter vibration in its transit, each *number* that touches the life.

No one key can unlock all doors, but at least you will be able to learn just when your periods of greatest accomplishment will occur and when you must either keep trying to adjust the key to the lock or wait patiently for the door to be opened from the other side. This vibration, like the Cornerstone, has a vital connection with the birthdate and here again it must be considered when changing the name, for its element may not be in harmony with the date of the birthday and may only induce more difficulties. The Key Number of the given name, if of the same element, may give too much of a good (or bad) thing (see the Chapter on the Four Elements); it may lessen oppositions, but it may also, like so many "trines" in the horoscope, eliminate the necessity for struggle, and therefore check real progress. If the Key is the *same* as the birthdate (that is, in actual number, but not in digit) the numbers are said to be "squared to each other" and there will be difficulty in unlocking the door—since the Key cannot fit a lock of exactly the same size. For example:— Your first name is Ann and you were born on the 11th.

ANN
1 5 5 = 11

The Expression of Ann, or your Key Number, is 11; your birthday falls on the 11th. 11 is an Air number (see Chapter on the Elements) and with both Key and Date in that Element, there would be a tendency to instability and superficiality: looked at from another angle, they are found to be the *same* number, therefore, not only can they not "transmute" each other, but the Key cannot unlock the door of the same size and they are "squared" to

every experience they contact that is out of their own element; they are "octaves" to each other.

J A M E S

1 1 4 5 1 = 12 = 3

born on the 4th would find the opportunities of his middle
Cycle somewhat limited and uninspirational, but JAMES,
through the Fire (3) of his Key Number would be *able*
to transmute those opportunities into expressions of force,
beauty and love: it would require ceaseless activity and
energy on his part, but he would have the *power* to unlock the door if he were willing to make the effort.

The sum or *essence* of the Key and birthday give what
is called the "Angle of Eccentricity" which is, as the
word implies, the peculiar, personal method of approach
to any situation. In the examples given above, the "Angle
of Eccentricity" or "Eccentric Angle" of Ann, born on the
11th, is 22 (or 4, if Ann chooses); that of James, born
on the 4th, is 7. As your own knowledge of the numbers
increases you will make many interesting comparisons and
deductions from your own Chart—always bearing in mind
the original meaning of any number and then the *shades*
of meaning of which it is capable in its different positions.

VOWELS

Vowels, the soul of a language, the soul-vibration of an
individual, are of the highest importance when seeking to
determine, by means of the *first* vowel of the name, the
first *spiritual* contact made with life.

Vowels are of three kinds, according to their *sound*. As
long (sometimes called broad), short, or as diphthongs

(in combination with other vowels) they are positive, receptive or dual. When long, or positive, the characteristics of the letter are emphasized and used in their full power; when short, or receptive, the power is less manifested, less outgoing in expression: when as diphthongs, their power is divided with the other vowel in association and the two are expressed in unison.

Vowels have a close affinity with health conditions and are subject to the rulership of the planets to which they are allied. For a *complete* understanding of the relationship between your first vowel and yourself, it is necessary to know its planetary correspondence on your own Chart. For all practical purposes, a thorough knowledge of Numerology will give us a sufficient guide with which to go through life, but all the sciences are closely inter-related, and the student who is eager for the last word in self-understanding should never be content with the mastery of one. Numerology and Astrology are the most closely related of the so-called "occult" sciences and each helps the other in character analysis, vocation and prognostication.

A

Review the general meanings and characteristics of A, and in particular its position on the "Planes of Expression." This holds good for all the vowels.

Positive—as in Mary, Sarah, James, etc.

As 1 it is creative, original and independent. As Fire it is Feeling. As a Mental-inspired letter it is concerned with the creative aspect on the mind-side. Those with A as a first vowel are progressive and adventurous; they must ever go forward, even at the cost of personal sacrifice; they must not be driven and will accept advice only as a confirmation of their own opinions. The positive A stands for Ambition and Aspiration; it is strong of will, opinionated, energetic, desirous of power and leadership and a lover of purity. If the surrounding vibrations are discordant or the birthdate out of harmony, the individual may express only negatively. The *power* is there, however.

Receptive—as in Patrick, Anne, Francis, etc. Less active and more poised. Inclined to dreaminess, idealism and sensitivity. Those having the receptive A often lack continuity and scatter the forces. If undeveloped they may become perverted. They are apt to feel frustrated and dissatisfied with life.

Dual—as in Daisy, Faith, Laura. The influence is fluctuating. They often pretend to be what they are not and one is reminded of the old limerick—

> *"There was a young lady named Maud*
> *Who was such a terrible fraud, that*
> *To eat at the table she never was able—*
> *But out in the pantry—O Lord!"*

If there are many A's in the name one is apt to be critical, cynical and sarcastic. The planetary ruler of A is Mars; * its inharmonious effect upon the health usually manifests in the form of headaches or brain congestion.

* The Planetary Rulership of the letters and the letters themselves have no *numerical* correspondence. The numbers of the letters are governed by one scale, the numbers of the Planets by another.

E

With E we may expect activity, contacts, travel, opportunity, motion, change, enterprise, agitation—commonly agitation in the soul.

Positive—as in Edith, Eva, Peter, Lena, etc. As 5 it has versatility, with scientific tendencies. As Air it is capable of thought on the spiritual plane. As a Physical-inspired letter it is concerned with invention and inspiration on the material plane. The positive E's are very practical, but full of progressive and illuminating ideas. They stand for Energy and Eventfulness.

Receptive—as in Jerry, Emma, Henry, etc. More poised and studious, or very restless and nervous. They are not aggressive, but are very determined and persistent. They are fond of dress and ornaments. If negative, they frequently lose their self-control.

Dual—as in George, Leila, Eoline. The nature is apt to be erratic and confused. These people interpret life experience in terms of their nervous reactions.

If there are many E's in the name one is apt to be restless, changeable and unstable. The planetary ruler of E is Venus; its effect upon the health is usually through the nerves of the stomach, causing indigestion and heartburn.

I

Intense emotional nature, force and vital energy. A law unto itself. I seems to be under the law of repetition and, if afflicted, "one woe doth tread upon another's heel, so fast they follow." It wants to perfect all its efforts and keeps repeating them.

Positive—as in Irene, Hiram, Silas, etc. As 9 it has artistic gifts, emotional understanding and universal interests. As Fire it is red-blooded and full of feeling. As an Emotional-inspired letter it is a passionate creator. I stands for Intensity. The positive I's are capable of greatness or crime. Heart and passion rule the mind. If developed, they are loving and serving; if not, self-indulgent and cruel.

Receptive—as in Isabelle, Imogene, Miriam, etc. Quiet, energetic, helpful—or erratic, uncontrolled and selfish. They are often very indifferent and bored.

Dual—as in Lionel, Diana, Violet, etc. Both seek expression—now the one, now the other.

Many I's make one touchy, sensitive but sympathetic. As a first vowel it is apt to bring about delays or static conditions. The planetary ruler of I is Saturn; it affects the health through the brain or the heart, producing insanity if greatly afflicted or if subjected to the Red Ray where the nature is violent. I is the killer or the genius; a broadcaster of terror or illumination.

O

Concentration and absorption, rest, poise, repose. Hidden beauty and power. Often bound to the dogmatic and traditional. Desire for personal power may obscure the mentality. May affirm and picture what it wants and succeed in attaining it. Strong, obdurate will, but yields completely if at all. Attracts grief through matrimony.

Suited to surgery and healing. Is sympathetic but re-strained, emotional but balanced. Does the best work at night.

Positive—as in Rose, Ora, Roland, etc. As 6 it is adjust-ing, responsible and helpful. As Air ($15 = 6$) it is devotional love; as an Emotional-inspired letter (and through its receptive qualities) it is capable of great illumination from its store of sympathetic counsel. The positive O's are gifted in music, poetry and art. If negative, may be domineering, arbitrary, selfish and unjust.

Receptive—as in Olive, Donald, John, etc. Emotional, sympathetic, enduring, protected. Often create images of inharmony and unpleasantness. If nega-tive, they are despondent and fault-finding.

Dual—as in Lois, Joan, Louise, etc. Great understanding of human nature and its frailties. Have difficulty in centralizing their own expression.

Too many O's incline to slowness, obstinacy and pig-headedness. As a first vowel it is apt to cause delay and slowness in decisions and movements. The planetary ruler of O is Jupiter; O affects the circulation and often pro-duces stasis.

U

Attracts peculiar and extraordinary forces, being open to all influences. It is conservative and does not seek the initiative. Highly intuitive, it often answers the *thoughts* of others and becomes garrulous for the purpose of con-cealing its own thoughts. It resists outside elements and strives to protect itself. It dislikes to ask questions and fears ridicule—therefore is slow in acquiring knowledge. The inherent idealism is usually beyond the execution. The life is much affected by strange and vivid dreams, which are frequent in occurrence. It attracts loss to itself.

Positive—as in Julia, Judith, Hubert, etc. As 3 it has artistic gifts, a love of light and an unwillingness to be alone. As Fire it is most concerned with feelings (its own). As an Intuitional-dual letter it is receptive (often clairvoyant) and vacillating. The positive U's are often tenacious and strive for accumulation and retention—fearing loss. They prefer a quiet, peaceful life and are very clannish and provincial. If well educated, they often incline to teaching or writing.

Receptive—as in Duncan, Dudley, Undine, etc. Very conservative in thought and action. If highly evolved, they strive to uplift the race; if not, they are selfish, narrow, miserly and secretive.

Dual—as in Quentin, Quincy, Guinevere, etc. Apt to be confused and are invariably aloof—therefore difficult to understand or, at the other end of the pole, over-free-and-easy in manner.

All U's are especially adapted for kindergarten work and the guardianship of children. If the intuitions are followed, there is protection, if not, invariably loss. The planetary ruler of U is the Moon. U affects the nerves and the spleen.

W *

The most difficult of letters. It has no place, strictly, in this classification, since W cannot be a *first* vowel; it is a vowel only when used in a diphthong and then *follows* another vowel. It is a strong force for good or ill; when completely inverted it becomes imbecility. It can, with difficulty, scale the heights, or, with greater ease, sound the depths. If undeveloped it is egotistic, conceited, self-ish, narrow, self-indulgent; if developed, a Master. As 5 it is *free* to go where it will; as Air it is capable of spirituality; as a Physical-dual letter it is unstable and vacillating on the material plane. It either aids the person to become worthy of a measure of fame or it holds him in limited circumstances. The planetary ruler of W is the Sun—explosive force in a lesser soul, great power in a great one. If afflicted, W gives general ill-health, produces malignant growths and induces shock.

Y

"The two paths." The left side of the letter is always broader than the right—the "narrow way." There is always an intuitional choice in Y—the heeding of the inner voice or the deliberate selection of the "primrose path." It may attain perfection through the reflective nature of its thought.

Positive—as in Myra, Byron, etc. As 7, the bridge between the two worlds, the desire for *hidden* truth

* W is actually the 7th vowel having been given a vowel significance *after* the introduction of Y. It needs, therefore, the special care in handling always demanded by the mysterious 7.

and the discovery of secret doctrines. As Water, it is much concerned with reflection and introspection. As an Intuitional-dual letter it is receptive but uncertain—reaching for guidance, receiving it, but still undecided about using it. The positive Y's must be left to their own decisions, guided only gently and loved much.

Receptive—as in Lydia, Myrtle, etc. These must be driven even less than the positive Y's and invariably treated with patience and reason.

Dual—as in Roy, Raymond, etc. (here not a *first* vowel, but a diphthong). Y being the weaker letter, will usually be overshadowed by the other vowel. It will contribute only duality and vacillation.

All Y's have great powers of perception in spiritual matters. They produce spiritual illumination or material tragedy. The planetary ruler of Y is Mercury—the higher vibration that rules reflective *thought*. Y induces ailments of the generative system and elusive, undiagnosed infirmities.

This concludes the intensive analysis of the letter vibrations of the name. Further references will be made, not only to the separate letters but to digits—as component parts and as finals, but the chapters immediately following will be concerned with the analysis of the full birthdate.

CHAPTER IX

THE CYCLES AND PINNACLES

THE word "Cycle" is a generic term. We speak of 7 as the Cosmic *Cycle*, 9 as the *Cycle* of Man, the *Cycle* of a letter (its transit) the *Cycle* of 9 years as sections or divisional parts of the life, and the *Cycles* behind the Life Path. In this chapter we are referring to the three great divisions of the Life Path, determined by the month, day and year of birth. These are the Cycles on the Path.

The Cycle of the month is first. This determines the Sun Sign under which the child is born and its *number* determines the influences under which the child will be during his entire youth and adolescence. The exact time of leaving one Cycle and entering another varies in individual cases, for here are Numerology and Astrology inextricably combined. No matter what the Personal Year number at the time, the first "Great Change" in the life occurs when the Progressed Moon, in the Astrological Chart, has completed its first revolution.

This actually happens at about the age of twenty-eight years and four months; youth and adolescence have passed and the young man or young woman is on the threshold of the flowering or middle Cycle of life. The individual may, however be in the *middle* of one of his "9-Year Sections" and if that is the case, not until he comes into his 1 Personal Year does the full effect of the change brought about by the Moon's revolution take full effect upon *him*.

Therefore, in figuring the time when you actually leave your first Cycle (the month) and pick up your second Cycle (the day) let it be determined by your 1 Personal Year *nearest* to the Moon's revolution, or *nearest* to your twenty-eighth birthday. A partial effect may be seen before that time, but its full meaning *for you* does not take effect until you start your new 9-year division with your 1 Personal Year.

The same rule holds for figuring the exit from the second Cycle (the day) and the entrance into the third and last (the year). The *second* revolution of the Moon takes the same time as the first—28 years and 4 months—and your 1 Personal Year *nearest* your 56th birthday will put you into your last Cycle on the Path.

Do not be satisfied with rules that are too general—as, for example, the division of your life into "quarter centuries"; the real divisions of your life are made by your stars and numbers *together*. You do *not* reach your second Cycle immediately after your 25th birthday nor your third immediately after your 50th—for your Moon does not work on the quarter-century plan. The Moon may cast its influence *ahead* of the 28th or 56th years, but you will be aware of its significance in the 1 Personal year *nearest* (before or after) those birthdays in your life.

The Cycles on the Path must always be treated as phases of the main direction to be followed—the Life Path itself—turns in the road which brings different types of the same experience. These phases must always be referred to the final number which is their sum, for our goal must never be lost sight of.

TABLE OF THE CYCLES

1

In this Cycle the individuality must be developed to the highest possible point. You must strive for independence, must develop your own resources and do no leaning on family or friends; you are to become the rock upon which others may lean. You must eliminate all fear and uncertainty, have the courage of your convictions and go straight ahead to the new and the progressive. You must use your powers of originality, creation and invention and make them work for you. You must seek the type of activity that calls for individual effort, seek to get to the top through your own efforts and make yourself indispensable to those with whom you come in contact. 1 is difficult as a first Cycle, for the child cannot be wholly independent and the result is usually a sense of isolation and the repression, by those in authority, of the very qualities that should be encouraged. As a middle Cycle it is best, for after 28 one should be capable of standing on his own feet—if ever. As a last Cycle it is somewhat more difficult as the requirement is constant effort and activity.

2

With 2 in the first Cycle, the child is apt to be badly spoiled. The emotions are on top and tears near the surface. If the Expression number is high, the child is liable to stutter, through feeling the difficulty of releasing a large content through a small vehicle. In the 2 Cycle you must learn adaptability and cooperation, attention to detail and obedience—serving in small ways willingly and harmoniously. You must seize and turn to account the smallest opportunity and there must be no insistence upon pushing the self to the front. It is a period of receptivity and collection rather than expression and all possible knowledge must be accumulated for future use. You must learn to be keenly aware of the feelings of others and cultivate patience, tact and diplomacy. Avoid personal sensitiveness but stress the kind of sensitiveness that stands between and *senses* the situation on both sides. As a middle Cycle it holds great opportunity for a diplomatic career (other things being equal). As a last Cycle you may still find yourself in politics and you will surely find yourself with an urge for collecting—pictures, art objects or property.

3

This is the Cycle of perfected self-expression. It should be a happy and carefree period, expressing on the lighter side of life. You should do much entertaining and embrace all opportunities to enlarge your circle of friends. This vibration is not friendly to learning, but rather to the expression of what has been already learned. You should enjoy life to the fullest and help others to do so. If you have any artistic talent, now is the time to encourage its expression. Use *words* on every possible occasion—write, speak, sing or act. You may also be successful at designing or decorating during these years. Your greatest help will come through social contacts. As a first Cycle 3 may be *too* expressive, and in any Cycle there is always danger of scattering the forces or indulging in things that are purely frivolous and unstable. As a middle Cycle it should certainly bring enjoyment of life; as a last Cycle, artistic activity and many friends.

4

This is the production period. You must not expect to do much playing, but must, instead, *work* at a definite task or submit to the limitation of the square. You must accept routine and learn to appreciate its value; you must keep in mind the ideal of service; you must practice economy and learn to make all things practicable and serviceable. As a first Cycle there is apt to be limitation or restriction of some sort—either financially or through the inability to express the ideals. As a middle Cycle, while the associates may be lacking in imagination and inspiration, the field limited and the opportunities for recreation and the cultivation of society small, you must remember that you are a *builder* and that one day your building will be finished and ready for occupancy. Never make the mistake of losing all ambition and plodding along in a rut; this can be one of the most valuable and foundation-laying periods of your life. As a last Cycle, 4 is not as fortunate as some of the numbers; but the appearance of the Work Number on a Chart does not always imply work *from necessity,* and you may be blest with the opportunity for doing a work you love. Always look at the Cycle that is ahead, until you come to the last; a Cycle *prepared for* loses all its terrors.

5

In this Cycle you must live with your trunks packed and your hat on. You will have change, uncertainty, variety, opportunity, travel, freedom and expansion. You will not be burdened with many responsibilities and should seek associations that will give you a new point of view. Avoid any tendency to settle down in one spot; if you are not uprooted from that spot by circumstances, uproot yourself, for your opportunity lies away from home and the usual routine. Pay much attention to your own charm and personal appearance. Keep up to date and move rapidly. Adapt yourself to everything that comes along. Learn a new language if possible. As a first Cycle the element of freedom is sometimes too great to be handled constructively; in this vibration are made the grave errors of "sex and the senses" so often deplored in later life. As a middle Cycle it means freedom and release from care; as a last Cycle, travel and pleasant variety.

6

Here you will be concerned with responsibility, domesticity and adjustment. As a first Cycle 6 may be restricting, for there is always a good deal of "chaperonage" connected with it, or there may be a heavy amount of home duties and responsibilities thrust upon you. As a middle Cycle 6 should mean your own home and happy family. As a last Cycle there is always protection and harmony to be found in this number—providing the need for *adjustments* does not press too heavily upon you. Restrictions and conventions must always be, to some extent, recognized in the 6, but the vibration will make it easier to live the lives of others and to help them bear their burdens. 6 is the best Cycle for marriage.

7

This is the period for the development of the inner resources. Nothing is to be actively *sought* from any personal or ulterior motive, but all that is in hand must be completed and perfected. Opportunity *comes* if not reached for, but flies if pursued. You must put all your mentality to use; study, meditate and grow wise. Emphasize in your life and work theories and fundamentals, learn peace and poise, understand the unseen while adapting yourself to exterior conditions. Form no partnerships, but avoid all pessimism and aloofness. Work alone if possible. As a first Cycle, the child usually suffers from repression and lack of understanding; he lives an inner life and is considered abnormal or difficult. As a second Cycle it is a wonderful period for the consideration of fine points and technicalities, for analysis and study. As a last period it usually leads one into philosophical fields or into some branch of research work. Marriage in a 7 Cycle is not to be recommended, since physical adjustments are difficult in this vibration.

8

In this Cycle you are concerned with the practical affairs of life—business, money and commercial activity. 8 is too high-powered for a first Cycle; it is usually the evidence of too much financial freedom for a child to understand and his lack of judgment in these matters becomes a handicap in later life. As a middle or last Cycle it is always constructive and there is always the possibility of great achievement. Assume direction and control and work for big results.

9

This is the most difficult of all as a first Cycle—as, in fact all the higher vibrations are harder for the child and easier for the adult. In the very early years, under the influence of 9, the child feels vague and frightened, nervous and decentralized—as though he were standing alone in the middle of a vast field. Later you become conscious of humanitarian principles and strive for selflessness in service. Cultivate tolerance, love, an acquaintanceship with the elevations of life. Work along the lines of art and further its message; feel no limitations; insist upon freedom. Do not become the victim of over-emotionalism and make every effort not to love too personally—for 9 belongs to the world and personal love-affairs do not thrive in its atmosphere. 9 is the end of a series, so marriage in this Cycle seldom lasts; that, and all other associations taken on during this period "finish" themselves. There is usually loss in the 9—a relinquishing of the purely personal.

11

As a first Cycle, the child will, inevitably, reduce the 11 to 2. Invention, inspiration and revelation thrive in the 11. Teach and inspire. The opportunities will come along artistic, emotional or inspirational lines. You have a great chance to make yourself famous while living under this influence. Do not try for expression in the commercial world for this is not the time for the ultra-practical or material. *Specialize* and hold fast to your ideals.

22

The high power of 22 will tax the nerves and resources. Assume leadership with all possible speed; seek only the large cooperative interests. Direct and manage. Listen for the Word and put it to practical use. Keep yourself always occupied and take up sculpturing as a side-line. Realize your ideals but keep your equilibrium.

THE PINNACLES *

The Pinnacles are found on the birth path and are the Essence of two Cycles whose influence is united or overlapping. As the Cycles represent the various circumstances, conditions and environment we find on the Life Path, the Pinnacles show us the "high spots" of our achievement in those conditions, our own reactions to them and the type of *events* we are likely to encounter as a result of the interaction of the Cycles. In this way the Pinnacles are highly prophetic and predictive and we may look ahead over the entire period of our lives and learn what we have to meet and how we may develop as we approach it. These are our peaks of attainment and carry the stamp we may put upon the years given us. Each succeeding Pinnacle may be prepared for ahead of time and during its operation we may reach the height of attainment indicated by its number.

It is often difficult to account for the changes that so unexpectedly take place in our affairs—our sudden ups and downs of fortune, or the sudden birth and death of

* The Pinnacles and the Challenge are the valuable contributions of Dr. Walton of California.

our various interests which gave promise of enduring throughout all time. We may find ourselves with an unaccountable change of attitude toward a line of work which we had labeled as a life-job, and suddenly we are no longer able to continue it or even tolerate the thought of it. Or we may have struggled for expression or success for a period of years and suddenly find ourselves wealthy or famous through the very thing we had despaired of.

All these changes are revealed by the Pinnacles, for they have a deep and subtle influence on the life and operate regardless of any other numbers we may be carrying. We may be down today, but next year may find us at the top—and *will* if we come into a Pinnacle of power; or we may, after enjoying years of luxury, suddenly find ourselves stranded in a hall-bedroom. The beauty of the Pinnacle-prediction is that there is no necessity for the hall-bedroom if you look ahead and see it coming; if you look *far* enough ahead you may prepare for it and turn it into a penthouse apartment.

There are four of these changes to be encountered as we go through life and they rise in peaks from the Cycles of the Path. The first and the last are longest in duration, for the first years of life, being formative and less manifesting, are slow in making their influence felt. The second and third rush rapidly along, having a period of nine years each—keeping pace with the rapidity of experiences that crowd upon the middle years of life. The last one picks it up at that point and endures to the end of life.

It will be seen that the Pinnacles do not run exactly parallel with the Cycles, but usually overlap into them; occasionally a Cycle and Pinnacle-change is made at the same time and that invariably brings into the life an important phase of experience.

Rule for Finding the Pinnacles

It has been said that there are four peaks of attainment to be found on the Path. Using 9 as the basic "Cycle of Man" number, that gives us 4 × 9, or 36 as a starting point. This 36, or total, however, must always be referred to the Life Path number and as it, in itself, has no part in the *calculation* of the Pinnacles we *subtract* the number of the Life Path from 36 in order to find the number of years of influence of the first Pinnacle. From there we go on to the next two periods of 9 years each, and from *that point* assign the 4th Pinnacle to the remaining years. This gives us the *duration* of each Pinnacle.

To find the *Pinnacle numbers* we proceed as follows:

FIRST PINNACLE.

Add together the digit of the month and the digit of the day. This number stands at the peak of the first upward-mounting triangle.

SECOND PINNACLE.

Add together the digit of the day and the digit of the year. This number stands at the peak of the second triangle, *beside* the first one.

THIRD PINNACLE.

Add together the numbers of the First and Second Pinnacles. This number stands at the peak of the third triangle which mounts upward from these two.

FOURTH PINNACLE.

Add together the digit of the *month* and the digit of the *year*. This is the all-embracing, all-enclosing triangle, starting from the lowest point and reaching to the top.

As an example we will set up the birthdate of George Washington.

We know that he was born Febuary 22nd, 1732, that his Life Path number was 1 and that his Cycles were 2, 22, 4. With our basis of 36 for the four Pinnacles, we must subtract 1 (the number of his Life Path) from 36 to find the duration of the first one, which is 35. The 2nd Pinnacle has a duration of 9 years and will last until he is 44 years old, the 3rd Pinnacle has a duration of 9 years and will last until he is 53; and the 4th or last Pinnacle will operate throughout the remainder of his life.

We now proceed to the Pinnacle numbers and for that purpose erect our triangles from the Cycles of the Path as follows:—

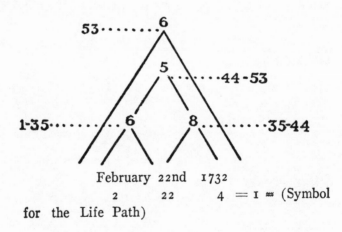

February 22nd 1732
2   22   4 = 1 ≋ (Symbol
for the Life Path)

The sum of 2 and 22 (4) = 6, the number of the first
    Pinnacle.
The sum of 22 (4) and 4 = 8, the number of the second
    Pinnacle.

The sum of these two, or 6 and 8 = 14 = 5, the number
of the third Pinnacle.

The sum of the month and year, or 2 and 4 = 6, the
number of the last Pinnacle.

From this diagram we know just what events came to
him at the periods of his life designated by the year-num-
bers at the side; also his own reactions and the type of
attainment possible in the various Pinnacles.

The First Pinnacle is always the most personal. This is
the start in life, when everything is referred to the self
and there is little concern outside of the immediate surroundings. As the Pinnacle overlaps into the second Cycle,
the concern becomes less personal and more *group*. The
birthday influence becomes a vital factor in the choosing of a vocation and, in accordance with the character
of the Pinnacle number will the events experienced help
or hinder early achievement.

The Second Pinnacle represents the period of obligation. The birthdate is still the most vital factor, but *age*
is to be taken into account, since the years are flying and
there is a necessity for working fast; the *year* of birth
lends its influence to the middle Cycle and forms the
second "peak" on the Path. Family and business responsibilities are increasingly important, together with many
other relationships and associations. Now must the foundation be laid for the top of the triangle, to be reached
within this 9-year period. There must be preparation
also for the more remote future, for powers and abilities
are at their height and there must be a measure of haste
before the next change.

In the Third Pinnacle we find the great prophetic indication. This is the content of all the Cycles—month, day and year. By this time the position in life is firmly established and the interests may be turned to wider fields and international concerns—if the unfoldment has been constructive and the peaks of attainment reached. The pace may be slower from now on, for a measure of leisure has been earned and one may feel relieved of the necessity for ceaseless concern with the "Great Without." The constructive individual will never choose to cease working or cease thinking, but the man or woman who has *attained* has a right to follow some of the pleasant by-paths of personal predilections or avocations by the time the third Pinnacle is reached. In this period, however, the foundation for the latter years must be well laid—and a knowledge of the number of the Fourth Pinnacle tells us exactly what sort of a foundation it should be.

The Fourth or Last Pinnacle drops out the whole hectic, middle period of life as a *manifesting* agent and concerns itself with the wisdom gained through retrospection and the vision of the future—the beginning and the end. This is the essence of the first and last Cycles—sometimes manifesting as a "second childhood," sometimes poor, lonely and unhappy—if preparation has been neglected and the consciousness of the universal unrealized. The just and always possible reward of the last Pinnacle is a broad and philosophic outlook, an active but not taxing occupation and well-earned peace and security.

In reading the Pinnacles several points must be borne in mind. Numbers have basic meanings which are unalterable, but the *positions* in which they are found give them shades and variations which produce vital differences in their *effects*. Pinnacles refer to events and inner reactions and not to places, environment or people. Their operation is inevitable and cannot be avoided; it can only be prepared for and then *met*. Their influences change at the exact times indicated by the individual Chart, although their peak of influence may not be reached until the 1 Personal year of the period under observation.

If the Number of a Pinnacle appears in the radical Chart (that is, the one set up with the full baptismal name and birthdate) it is especially significant and its meaning is intensified. For example: If your Soul Urge number is the same as one of your Pinnacle numbers, when you come under the influence of that Pinnacle events will come into your life that will be in accord with your heart's desire. Or if your Pinnacle number tallies with your Expression, you will find every response and assistance along the lines of your abilities. Or if your Pinnacle number is the same as your Life Path, you will find opportunity provided not only for your activities but for the easy and painless assimilation of the lessons required of you. By the same token, if the Pinnacle Number is the same as one of your Karmic Lessons, if that lesson has not already become a part of your Subconscious, you will find the period a difficult one.

Knowledge is the first protection, preparation the second, eager acceptance of the vibration the third.

TABLE OF THE PINNACLES

1

Activity, change, a chance to individualize. Inner response—the cultivation of independence and the refusal of repression.

2

Not forceful, but cooperative and accumulative. Inner response—the cultivation of diplomacy and harmonization.

3

Pleasant, cheerful events, creative and artistic stimulation. Inner response—cultivation of the arts and the development of the talents. WORDS.

4

Slow moving and sure building; a chance to prepare for the future. Inner response—patience, service and non-resistance.

5

Many experiences, frequent change, matters of foreign interest, publicity. Inner response—discard of the old, expansion, *readiness*.

6

Responsibilities, adjustments, home, duties, love, burdens. Inner response—harmonization, accord, service, love.

7

Philosophy, analysis, fundamentals, religion, seclusion, possible lack of material benefits, knowledge. Inner response—poise, self-examination, waiting.

8

Attainment, authority, success, recognition. Inner response—cultivation of balance and judgment, courage, growth.

9

Completion, breadth, greatness, disappointment in personal matters, reward in universal. Inner response—love, sympathy, selflessness.

11

Spiritual expansion, illumination, fame, nervous tension. Inner response—Holding the ideals, cultivation of inventive ability.

22

International concern, world affairs. Inner response—expansion of consciousness.

CHAPTER X

THE CHALLENGE

THE Challenge is a sign-post on the Life Path. It carries a red flag and its inscription is "Danger Ahead!"

Being an emanation of the Birthdate, it is a quality of consciousness which becomes a part of the individual with the first intake of breath, and is an indication of the hazards presented by the individual Cycles. In contradistinction to the Pinnacles, whose triangles mount *upward* to development and expansion, the Challenge-triangles point *down* to the material plane of manifestation and show the weak links to be strengthened for success and happiness in *material* affairs and *external* relationships.

The Challenge is a staff to help us over the steep places on the Path. It is a merciful dispensation from the birth forces, a definite guide to the feet which *must* take a certain direction, but which might easily stumble into certain pitfalls along the route. There is no impossible leap to be taken; no task to be met that is beyond our handling; we are given to do only what we are able to do, and the Challenge shows what to strengthen or modify that we may see a clear road ahead.

Every nature, no matter how strong or capable, has within its depths some weakness, some inhibition or some flaw. Certain vibrations bring with them certain difficulties and it is only through the inner consciousness that these may be dealt with. The Challenge tells us exactly what these difficulties are, and we have only to study the NUMBER held up before us and bend our wills and energies toward its constructive expression to see the difficulties melt into thin air.

Like a dangerous pitfall or landslide, this vibration is often so deeply hidden that we are not aware of its existence until it looms large and unconquerable before us. The kindly Challenge appears to tell us in advance. Heeding its warning once or twice, however, is not enough: the barrier it represents may appear at any moment throughout the entire life, and since it represents the particular type of weakness to which the individual is prone, must be kept *constantly* in mind until it is so built into the consciousness that the fault becomes an asset. When this is accomplished, the life is brought into the channels of power and progress and lack of friends, funds, opportunity and success become things of the past.

Like the vibration of the Life Path, the *final* number of the Challenge is the major indication, but like the Cycles, the numbers *behind* the final digit show the qualities that must be emphasized during the periods from which they are derived—that is, the first division, or "sub-Challenge" operates during the first Cycle and a part of the second; the second sub-Challenge during the remainder of the second Cycle and into the third—and the final Challenge *always*.

Look upon the Challenge as a lantern to be kept filled and lighted at all times. If it is not trimmed and burning, we find ourselves in the dark; if we carry it lighted before us, we cannot lose the way.

RULE FOR FINDING THE CHALLENGE

The Challenge is found from the Life Path. The rule of subtraction is used. In the case of the Master Numbers, 11 and 22, they are reduced before subtraction.

1st: Subtract the digit of the month and the digit of the day from each other. (The result gives the first sub-Challenge.)

2nd: Subtract the digit of the day and the digit of the year from each other. (The result gives the second sub-Challenge.)

3rd: Subtract these two remainders from each other. The result gives the *final* Challenge.)

For example:

We will again set up the birthdate of George Washington.

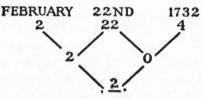

We first subtracted the digit of the month (2) and the digit of the day (22 = 4) from each other. This gave us 2 as the first sub-Challenge.

We then subtracted the digit of the day (4) and the digit of the year (4) from each other. This gave us 0 as the second sub-Challenge.

We then subtracted these two results from each other (0 from 2 = 2). This gave us the final Challenge for the Birth Path of George Washington.

(The symbol · — · is used for convenience).

TABLE OF THE CHALLENGE

1

Tendency to negative resistance. Much opposition will be met with. *Things* will interfere with the desires; people (usually relatives) with stronger wills will try to control the life. You will find yourself vacillating and uncertain as to which way to turn—often because of a laudable desire to please everybody. You will end by pleasing nobody—least of all yourself. The Inclusion Table must be carefully studied and the number of 1's noted, for the 1-Challenge *may* indicate self-insistence and self-promotion.

(It is practically impossible to make definite assertions about the Challenge. Like all the vibrations, it is an individual matter, but it is more *personal* than the others and deals not so much with inherent qualities as with the handling of situations arising from material concerns. The *application* of the Challenge can be accurately made only by the individual; he must familiarize himself with both sides of the number, and then ask himself which side he is over- or under-working).

Remedy—Strengthen your will-power. The creative and daring 1 is as valuable in this position as elsewhere. First make sure you are right and then go straight ahead—not pugnaciously, but firmly. Or: Cease thinking that the world does (or should) revolve about yourself. Whether your weakness is vacillation or pig-headedness, ask yourself daily, after looking at the Number 1—
What am I doing about this?

2

This is the Challenge of sensitiveness. You are making yourself miserable by referring everything to your own feelings and emotions. You are in danger of becoming petty and small-minded through the minute and detailed 2. *Little* things of life appear as insurmountable obstacles and they hurt and hinder you at every turn. You are so open to every influence that you follow the most recent example or impression and base your life upon imitation. You refuse to forgive or forget the thoughtless words of others. You find it difficult to work with others because you seem so important to yourself you would rather not run the risk of being hurt or slighted by them. You have forgotten the lessons of good manners, kindliness and consideration drummed into your early years, for the simple reason that the feelings of others matter very little in comparison with your own.

Remedy—Stop referring everything to yourself. Cultivate a broader outlook on life. Don't imitate others: Be yourself. Throw hesitation, indecision and fear out of your life. OR:
Through your desire to keep the peace, don't forget to tell the truth. Just because you want to be nice, don't be an insincere flatterer. If you have become aware of the beautiful psychic power in your 2, don't try to commercialize it. Look at your Challenge and ask yourself—

> Am I a door-mat?
> " " " prevaricator?
> " " " sensitive cry-baby?
> " " afraid of my own shadow?
> AM I MYSELF?

3

Obstacles in the way of Expression have been allowed to stunt its growth. You are burying your talents in a napkin. Look at your Inclusion and see if an excess of 2's and 4's are not interfering. In spite of your personal inclination for self-effacement and your aversion to society and the lighter side of life, if you do not force yourself into the cultivation of the gifts of "3", you are going to be in sore need of social contacts, music, art, beautiful clothes, a happy disposition and WORDS. Occasions will arise when care of the personal appearance will turn the scales for or against you; when your lack of eloquence will make you unable to put over your proposition, or when your inability to be a welcome addition to a social gathering—to dance, sing, play or act—will make you lose the opportunity of the moment.

Remedy—Stop being such a mouse and become more of a butterfly. No matter how old you are, learn to do some of the things that give you a good time; take up dancing, singing, fencing or public speaking—and watch yourself blossom out into a new plant. OR:— Take life rather more seriously and stop wasting so much time in frivolity. Chatter less and avoid gossip altogether. Don't spend all your money on clothes and ornaments.
  Questions:—
    Am I a recluse or a fly-by-night?
    Am I unduly extravagant?
    Am I moody and cranky?
    Am I a waster of words or do I eschew them altogether?

4

This Challenge is perhaps the easiest of all, in one sense— for its admonition is to Pay Attention, and there is no emotional conflict involved. The 4-Challenge may warn us that we are in danger of being lost in a maze of detail; that we are straight-laced, hide-bound and intolerant; that we are wedded to custom and not amenable to progress; that we are working in a rut and forgetting all necessary play. Or, as is more frequently the case, we are lazy and inattentive; careless about details and appointments; lose or mislay the things that should have been put in their proper places; refuse to work with concentration or system; waste where we should conserve; scatter when we should accumulate, force issues instead of waiting for them to ripen—in short, we hate WORK.

Remedy:—Put *everything* away as soon as you have finished with it. Put yourself on a schedule and keep to it. Avoid all inclination to be lazy. Get up earlier than is your custom. Answer all letters within three days. Buy a file, an address book, an account book and a diary—and use them.
Questions:—
>   Am I rigid, set and stubborn?
>   Am I lazy, careless and impractical?
>   Are the *corners* dusty?

5

This Challenge has a twofold meaning; the first deals with sex and the senses—the misuse or abuse of the freedom in the 5: the second deals with Discard,—freedom from another angle—the freedom we give to things or people by letting go of them. We either obey the law or disregard it; we may scale the heights or plumb the depths; we may progress in expansion or run around in circles. This is one of the most difficult Challenges, for here you must learn to understand *when* to change and to *what*. A distinction must be made between the healthy type of restlessness that wants to progress, gain more knowledge and make more contacts and the type that flits from one thing to another from mere love of change and distraction—refusing to stabilize, burning all bridges behind him. The pitfall on the sex-side is the result of the same seeking, eager quality—the urge to satisfy an impulse or ideal as soon as it arises—to seek an outlet as an *experiment*. With the 5 vibration the senses are always uppermost; they want to leave nothing untried; drink, drugs, "whoopee" are so many experiences offered by life —everything must be tasted and judged. Speed, impulse and curiosity all stand ready to overthrow the one with 5 on the Challenge.

Remedy—Restrain that impulse to try *everything* at least once. Don't be so eager to pass on to the next thing until you have satisfied the obligations of the thing in hand. Stay long enough in one place or at one job to know what there is in it. Don't cast aside your old friends or loves like so many worn-out shoes.

Questions:—
Is my curiosity about life sound and healthy?
Do I cling to old conditions when I should pass on to new?
Do I try to hold my friends when they are ready to go?
Do I rule my impulses or do they rule me?

6

This is the Challenge of distorted idealism—beware of it! 6 is full of ideals and principles, knows the law (as he sees it) and wants everyone to accept it—according to *his* interpretation. In the Challenge-position 6 is exacting and domineering, eternally striving to jack everyone up to his standards and meeting with one disappointment after another because no one ever quite comes up to specifications. If he allies himself with an organization whose officers do not seem to *him* irreproachable, he will either quarrel with them, or leave. If he marries, and his wife does not do things according to *his* methods, he will leave home or get a divorce. He is over-positive about right and wrong and never tolerates any deviation from the rules he has set down. He never makes any mistakes, but everybody else makes many. All the love, harmony and adaptability of the 6 become lost in the fog of self-opinion and self-righteousness. He is *smug*.

Remedy—Realize that life is an *individual* problem and don't attempt to make rules for anybody except yourself. If you cannot adjust or ameliorate conditions you meet with, either go away from them or shut your eyes to them if you are too involved to leave. If you aren't in a position to make laws, don't worry about every newspaper report of prevailing conditions and harp on your favorite note, "There ought to be a law," etc. You will never find the love and companionship so necessary to your happiness until you learn to respect another's point of view and cease trying to re-make it to fit your own.

Questions:—In my passion for making adjustments, am I able to adjust *myself* to conditions in my own home?

Do I allow my wife (or husband) to have her own standards and opinions?

Have I an idea that I could run the home, the office or the Universe better than it is being run at present?

Am I a self-righteous prig or a balanced and harmonious 6?

7

This is the Challenge of Repression—the most tragic of them all. You may be the victim of one of two extremes— either an ungovernable pride or an unreasoning self-effacement. You may have a sterling character, but if you insist upon standing aloof from life *as it is given you to live,* you cannot expect happiness in human relationships or success in mundane occupations. You will find yourself in constant rebellion against existing conditions—making no effort to better them (through hopelessness or inefficiency) and unwilling to stand out as a pioneer on a trail that leads to better things. You are constantly at war with yourself—seething and decentralized within, or yielding to the ever-lurking curse of 7—Drink. There is a secret or hidden condition to be overcome.

Remedy—Give yourself as good an education as is humanly possible. Use your fine technical and spiritual qualities of 7 in the open instead of turning them in upon yourself. Force yourself to an understanding of the things transpiring outside of your own enclosure. Cultivate faith in the beauty and justice of the general plan. Relinquish the bogies of poverty, loneliness and failure for your old age. Hold fast to the *realities*.

Questions:—

Am I indifferent and aloof?

Do I have fits of melancholia and despair that render me unfit for ordinary society? and that occasionally drive me to drink?

Do I realize that my limitations are self-imposed and unnecessary?

Does my 7 give me Faith or Fear?

8

This is the Challenge of material affairs and means disregard or over-emphasis in their direction. Wastefulness is often as destructive as cupidity and miserliness, but the usual warning of the 8-Challenge is the danger of strain after money and power. Personal freedom becomes a fetish and 8's are in danger of thinking that the only way it can be gained is by the accumulation of money and possessions. A false sense of values rules the life and the constant fear of limitation usually succeeds in inviting it.

Remedy—Stop thinking eternally about money and what it can do for you. Look over the list of millionaires and ask yourself if you would honestly prefer to be in their shoes rather than your own. Try and recall the number of cases where money has brought happiness. Realize that MONEY has a Soul Urge of 9 and an Expression of 9—which means that it belongs to *everybody* and will spell LOSS when its acquisition becomes a purely personal matter. Let go of your attitude of *strain* toward it, obey the laws that govern it and you will find it dropping into your lap as the result of your determination to keep your mind on the job instead of the pay-envelope.

Questions:—

Am I making a god of dollars and cents?

Will all my reasons for wanting money bear the light of day?

When I get it, just how am I going to use it?

Do I deserve to have it and can I be trusted to do the right
thing by it and with it?
Do I realize that I must understand 7 before I can handle 8?

The 8-Challenge appears only in connection with the o.
If o is the *first* sub-Challenge, the result is usually a self-
made man; if the 8 is the first its importance is so emphasized that one is in danger of becoming mercenary.
8 as the final Challenge always warns us to cultivate a
constructive attitude toward true values and the right use
of power—or be undone by the very thing we have most
set our hearts upon.

9

This number does not appear on the Challenge. 9, being
the highest number, cannot be subtracted from and still
remain 9.

o

Because the o gives us no definite indication of what
must be strengthened or avoided, this is, perhaps, the
most puzzling of all the Challenges. We can get some
help from the sub-challenges that lie behind, but of the
exact warning implied in the cipher we have no indication. Generally speaking, it is the Challenge of *Choice*.
No burden is ever put upon shoulders unfit to carry it,
and if you find an o Challenge on your Path, you may
know that you have reached a point in your evolution
when you may be trusted to choose for yourself. In its
very symbolism, it goes back to the origin of all things—
the All before there was the 1. You are to make your own
decisions about life and are expected to *know* where your
pitfalls lie. To successfully meet the o ‿‿u will need a

knowledge of all the vibrations—the Independence of the 1; the Diplomacy of the 2; the Optimism of the 3; the Application of the 4; the Understanding of the 5; the Adjustment of the 6; the Wisdom of the 7; the Constructive Power of the 8; the Universal Service of the 9. Out of these you may create your own world and rise to great heights—from 0. Or, having *All* within the 0, you may descend as far in the other direction. You must earn your own rewards, but for that purpose you have all the necessary equipment.

Eternal Vigilance—in all directions—is the Challenge of the 0. Minor guides may be found in the Sub-Challenges, but the main sign-board bears the one word, CHOICE. If you have 0 on the Challenge you *know* which way to turn; but you must *know* that you know and then—Choose.

1, 2, 3, and 0 are the most commonly found Challenge Numbers, showing that the majority of people are meeting the same barriers in life. Some are more aware and therefore better able to cope with them, but most of us are in the same grade. For that reason we should be careful in making our judgments, for we may be on the same level of consciousness in our relation to universal life.

4 and 5 come next in frequency—6 more rarely.

7 is very rare and the most difficult to carry.

8 is found only in conjunction with the 0.

9 is not found. 0, from the spiritual viewpoint, is equal to 9.

CHAPTER XI

CHOOSING THE VOCATION

THE title of this chapter is a misnomer. The Vocation is a true summons or Calling (from the Latin *vocare,* to call) and there is no question of choice; we simply answer the summons. The majority of people, however, are not so fortunate as to be definitely called to a certain type of work and must make the decision for themselves.

In making this decision many things must be carefully considered and probably the most important of these is the Expression. While the Expression does not represent the sum of *all* our capabilities, it gives the clue to what we most easily and naturally *can* do for it sums up the things with which we have had experience in the past and are, therefore, most familiar. This must be immediately referred to the Cornerstone and Key Number, for if the foundation upon which we build our Expression is not adapted to its requirements, the whole structure will be shaky; and if the Key does not fit the lock of the door we are daily passing through, one or the other must be changed for the sake of security.

Soul Urge and Ruling Passion may have to be excluded at first. What we *can* do does not always coincide with what we *long* to do or with what we find the most pleasure in doing; if it does, so much the better, for then we shall put our whole souls into the job at hand and get a lot of fun out of it at the same time. We must consider our equipment rather than our desires and *then* our Opportunity.

The Life Path, as we know, is the *only* direction for us to go and only there shall we find the chance to market our wares. So we have, thus far, the Abilities and the Opportunities.

The next point to consider is the birthdate. Since this number is on the Path of Requirement we are *subject* to its influence and obliged to respond to its active and positive force. This is the first great factor in the department of Tendencies. For other tendencies we turn next to the Planes of Expression and discover our place of power. Place each letter of your name under its own sub-head on its own Plane and then add together all the letters of the Mental, the Physical, the Emotional and the Intuitional to see in which one of the four main divisions you have the greatest force. Then go *across* the Table and make an addition of all the Inspired numbers, all the Dual and all the Balanced. The next step of importance is to note the first vowel of your name.

We may now pass on to the Preferences. The first number to be considered is the Soul Urge; we would like to find a place for it and *shall* if the "Vocation" is to be a life-work; if it must be chosen from motives of expediency or necessity, the Soul Urge may not be able to enter into it, but if it does not, the work will lack the spark of vitality and heart-interest that would otherwise make it permanent. If we find no place for the Soul, we may be able to fit into the scheme the Ruling Passion; that will help to keep it going through our own interest and fondness for it.

We may next look at the Possibilities. Perhaps we have been unable to relate our Capabilities, Opportunities, Tendencies and Preferences to each other, so we have a second choice in what we *might* go in for successfully. For this information we return to the Inclusion Table and note the strength and weakness of the various vibrations. One of our "inclusions" may indicate the very line in which we might prove highly proficient.

We must now consider the present influences and these we find in the Cycles and Pinnacles and, to a lesser extent, in the Personal and Universal Year.

We must never lose sight of the Barriers (Karmic Lessons and Challenge) and must realize that, whatever line of work we choose, they are always stalking by our side like so many ghosts until "laid."

We may summarize these Vocational Guides as follows:—

1. ABILITIES

Look at your Expression Number. Does it belong to the "Great Within" or the "Great Without"—that is, do you most readily express along the lines of art or business?
Look at your Cornerstone. Note its number and its letter; see on what Plane the letter belongs and what its classification on its own Plane. Are you *built* upon Mind, Body, Feeling or Spirit?
Look at your Key Number. What is its Element? Is it in harmony with your Expression?

2. OPPORTUNITIES

Look at your Life Path. Is it odd or even ("Within" or "Without")? Is it in harmony with your Expression?

What is its Element? Is it in or out of concord with your Key and Corner? Is one of the numbers able to "transmute" the other? How will they affect the type of work you have in mind?

3. TENDENCIES

Look at your birthdate. What kind of a person are you, inherently, according to this birth requirement?

Look at your Planes of Expression. Do you find yourself strongest on the Mental Plane and are still contemplating manual labor? Or are you Emotional-dual and think you can fit a post of great responsibility?

Look at your first Vowel. Are you a Positive A and expect to thrive in a subordinate position? or are you a Receptive E and expect to fill a position where self-control and attention to routine are the prime requisites?

4. PREFERENCES

Look at your Soul Urge. Are you an artist in the Soul and looking for happiness in a manufacturing concern? Or are you an efficient executive and are contemplating a clerkship in an Antique Shop?

Look at your Ruling Passion. Do you love your freedom above everything else and think you can get any enjoyment out of punching a time-clock? or do you really enjoy system, detail and order and think of accepting a post as companion to a society woman?

5. POSSIBILITIES

Sum up everything you have or haven't analyzed before—especially the indications of the Inclusion and Planes. If your 1's, 4's and 7's are weak, don't expect to succeed at the mental, responsible, analytical or technical jobs. If you have many 6's, try nursing, care of children or institutional work. If you are strong in 3, get into the atmosphere of decorating, designing or dressmaking. If you have many 9's and can find no place in the arts, try for social welfare work.

6. Present Influences

Look at your present Cycle. Note the type of people, conditions and environment it will give you, and the sort of help you will receive from them. See how much longer you will be in this Cycle.

Look at your present Pinnacle. Note the experiences you are going to have during its operation and take into account your own reactions. Note carefully the number of the *next* Pinnacle and see how you can best prepare for it.

Look at your Personal Year and the Universal. Fit your contemplated choice to the general need, but consider your own angle. If this is a *new* job and you are in a 9 Personal Year, don't expect it to last.

7. Barriers

Look at your Karmic Lessons. Don't choose the type of work where you will constantly be brought face to face with them unless you have learned them; you will only be increasing your own difficulties.

Look at your Challenge. If it is 2, don't go in for Diplomacy unless you are sure of yourself; if it is 4 don't take on the handling of intricate detail and system.

In every instance, consult the lists and Tables from each of these angles, to determine the type of work which you are best fitted to engage in. The majority of people are not specialists or geniuses and therefore find it necessary to change their occupations from time to time as varying influences come into their lives. Adapt all you can to what you can. You cannot expect to find a "perfect fit" of each part to every other.

CHAPTER XII

TESTING NUMBERS. THE TRIADS

Colors and Musical Tones

The Numbers of the Planets

THERE are four "Testing" or "Warning" Numbers—
often called "Malefics." *No* number is evil; if its effects
are unfortunate and difficult, we have only to remember
that we are reaping the rewards of our own past performances and that the Law says we must pay for all we
get and for whatever harm we do. The same Law, however, pays, on the other side of the book, for every effort
in the right direction.

Each of the Testing Numbers bears a message of
Karma to be satisfied, quite apart from the Karmic Lessons that appear in the Inclusion Table. Usually we can
see the evidence of our debt in the present life—but not
always. A knowledge of the meaning of each Testing
Number will enable us to handle it the more efficiently
and not repeat the former mistakes. They are all symbols
of reconstruction and we may win through to a higher
level by due regard to their significance.

The numbers are 13, 14, 16, and 19.

13

(Not always listed with the Testing Numbers.) Its origin
probably dates back no farther than the Christian Era,

to the Last Supper, where 13 were present and One died. Anciently, 13 was one of the most highly revered numbers, but considered so holy and unapproachable that it began to be feared and shunned. Thoughts of destruction have come down with it through the ages and all sorts of superstitions have been built around it. To the true occultist it is a number of power and divinity; to the layman it is one to be avoided. If it has any destructive power it is because of the negative thought surrounding it for so many centuries. For those who have mastered it, it is constructive and fortunate. Its sum is 4, but behind it is the 1 and the 3—insistence upon the Path of Dalliance when the goal is work and construction. Its warning is the danger of backsliding into laziness and negativity. One must learn to step from triviality into a 4-square type of construction. Its slogan is WORK on the material plane. Its title is

TRIALS AND TESTS OF PROFICIENCY

14

Called the Number of Mars—destructive, bound up in reincarnation. It is difficult for a 14-5 to remember and profit by experiences. It is deeply absorbed in things of the senses—therefore the Destroyer on the physical plane. It delays results; brings loss, sickness, sudden death or deformities. (A hunchback with 14 shows too much former saturation with physical appetites.) It clings to physical sensations.

If found in the Soul Urge—It warns of interruption in all emotional affairs.

If found in the Expression—It warns of disappointed hopes
and a new balancing of forces.

"   "   on the Life Path—A lesson to be learned—to
have, to hold and then let go.
14 must learn the Law of
Change; must gain and use
freedom rightly.

    Its title is—WATERS OF LETHE.

16

This is the test for the faith and optimism of 7. The
"Temple of Spirit" is the only safe dwelling place for 16.
The power of Spirit is all that can keep the Tower from
falling (see the 16th Tarot card). 16 can reach the 7-digit
only through crucifixion of the self (the 1) on the cross
of love (the 6). 16 is the Karma of former illegitimate
love.

If found in the Soul Urge—It warns of broken dreams (or
heart), false friends and mis-
alliances.

"   "   "   " Expression—Loss of name, place, position,
power, fortune.

"   "   on the Life Path—All tragedies must be learned
—rise to fall, love to lose,
hold to let go.

    Its title is—THE FALLING TOWER OF URANUS.

19

The Number of Saturn. 19 is the Collector of Taxes and
demands Measure for Measure. This is evidence of power
formerly misused. The final Karmic debts must all be

paid before the completion of the Life Cycle. Formerly, something was taken from the Universe that was not paid for. If paid speedily, one is freed from the "Circle of Necessity"; if refused, debt is piled upon debt—ultimately to pay up. Called the vibration of endurance— How much can we stand?

If found in the Soul Urge—Tests of Life and Death. Leads us to the grave and bids us look across to the beginning of life. All the life secrets are dragged to the light.

"   "   "   " Expression—We may find ourselves stripped at the finish of the race.

"   "   on the Life Path—We must reap what we have sown. We struggle with the burdens of the past. We are bound when we want to be free. We must pay with time, money and ourselves.

Its title is—THE RISING SUN OF A NEW DIS-PENSATION.

(See the 19th Tarot card.)

────────

THE TRIADS

Certain numbers, because of inherent relationships, form triads of classification that seem to follow a certain mathematical and musical law.

1-4-7 are the *Angular* numbers and form the Mental Triad. In this group the expression may show many vital differences, as in the Inspiration of 1, the Form of 4 and the Spiritual Analysis of 7, but the concern is always mental and the process always of the mind.

3-6-9 are the *Triangular* numbers, being all emanations of the basic Trinity. These numbers express emotionally, in art forms.

2-5-8 are the *Curved* numbers, because of the duality inherent in their inmost natures. They are concerned with outward expression.

This same law is found in the geometric progression of superimposed triangles and in the interval-relationships of the musical scale.

Colors and Musical Tones

Color is sound made visible—or sound on a higher plane, at a higher rate of vibration. This gives us a close correspondence between the three forms of vibration with which we are most familiar—Color, Tone and Number.

Many musicians have recognized color as "visible sound" and thought of acceleration as "blue," of wild storms as "red," of serene and lofty heights as "violet," of pastorales as "green." Liszt, Meyerbeer, Schumann, Hans von Bülow and many others talked and worked in terms of color.

Pythagoras, the Father of Number, first discovered the diatonic scale, and based his original experiments on the universal principle of 7—the cosmic number. The 7 tones have their correspondences in the 7 colors of the spectrum, the 7 Planets and the first 7 or *bound* numbers.

Using Middle C as the first note of the scale, we find it has many points in common with 1—it is creative, aggressive and progressive. The color of 1 or C is RED.

D, or 2 is a great departure from 1 (the 1 beside the 1) but it is also the mediator between 1 and 3. The color of 2 or B is ORANGE.

E or 3 is the expression of light, beauty and sympathy. The color of 3 or E is YELLOW.

F or 4 is the builder for the completion or manifestation of further expression. The color of 4 or F is GREEN.

G is the restless, seeking 5, powerful in itself but obliged to *move on* to something else. The color of 5 or G is Green-BLUE.

A or 6 is deep, vital, balanced. The color of 6 or A is INDIGO.

B is the mysterious, subjective 7; it does not fully reveal itself but gives the impression of holding, within its own depths, many secrets that we need to know. The color of 7 or B is VIOLET—the last color of the spectrum—the bridge to the "other side."

The primary colors are Red, Yellow and Blue; the Tonic Chord is 1, 3, 5.

The half-tones of the Scale have the colors between the basic 7, and in the complete scale the colors are as follows:—

C —Red
C#—Red-orange
D —Orange
D#—Orange-yellow
E —Yellow
F —Yellow-green
F#—Green
G —Green-blue
G#—Blue

A —Blue-purple (indigo)
A♯—Purple
B —Violet (tinged with the red of the higher C)

Play your own chords as found in your Soul Urge, Expression and Life Path. Find the Keynotes of your principal vibrations and play upon them the harmonies to which they respond. Your Soul wants its own music; your Expression will be more vital and harmonious because of it; your Life Path will send the opportunities that respond to its vibration.

The color of 8 is rose, or the higher vibration of red (1).

9 is the epitome of all the colors or the aura that surrounds them all. Use yellow-gold for 9; it is the light of the Sun.

11 is pure silver; 22 red-gold—the light of the Sun mixed with the clay of the Earth.

Wear the color of your Soul Urge for relaxation and for dreaming.

Wear the color of your Expression to vitalize your capabilities.

Wear the color of your Life Path to attract new opportunities.

GEMS

1—Rubies
2—Moonstones
3—Topaz
4—Emeralds
5—Turquoise
6—Pearls or Sapphires
7—Amethysts or Aqua Marines
8—Diamonds
9—Opals
11—Platinum
22—Coral or Red Gold

THE NUMBERS OF THE PLANETS

```
SUN ............... 1
MOON ............. 2
VENUS ............ 3
SATURN .......... 4
MARS ............. 5
JUPITER .......... 6
MERCURY ......... 7
SUN .............. 8
NEPTUNE ..........11
URANUS ..........22
```

9 is again the "Aura" and has no Planet peculiar to itself; it is the consummation of all their influences.

The Sun is fire—the Beginner and Instigator—the creative 1.

The Moon is the adaptable, mediating 2, ruler of the tides.

Venus, as 3, is Fire—but also *Earth,* inasmuch as Earth is the crystallization of Fire; Earth transmuted is Fire itself. They are closely related, as the positive and negative poles of their generating element. Venus is also one of the many aspects of love—*artistic* love, and not the unchanging, devotional love of 6.

Saturn holds and crystallizes. Like all 4's, he represents form and discipline which, when met and profited by, bring sure and permanent rewards.

Mars is the active, seeking, changing 5—warlike and destructive or creative and expansive.

Jupiter rules the two aspects of the 6—the protective, material love and well-being (Earth-side) and the transmuted devotion of its higher side (Air).

Mercury rules the mental 7. The *explosive* qualities of Mercury rule the unpoised, talkative 7; the positive

Mercury, like the positive 7, never expresses himself unwisely. As an Air Planet, Mercury transmutes the Water of 7.

8 is again the Sun—the octave of 1; 11 is ruled by the dreamy, visionary Neptune—impractical, mysterious, illuminating; to 22 is given the tremendous electrical force of Uranus—the power of the destruction of form for the purpose of its reconstruction.

CHAPTER XIII

COMPARISONS AND ASSOCIATIONS IN MARRIAGE, FRIENDSHIP AND PARTNERSHIP

CITIES, TOWNS AND COUNTRIES

THERE are two ways of making comparisons:

(1) In the Individual Chart, among the principal numbers.

(2) In two Charts, to determine harmony or inharmony in association.

The advantage of making comparisons in the Chart of the individual is to determine where the adjustment must be made or, if seemingly impossible to harmonize the vibrations, to make a change in the name. These comparisons cannot fail to result in a more complete understanding of the equipment.

In the Personal Chart there are three main factors to be noted:—

1. What are the Elements? Are they congenial or unfriendly?
2. Are the numbers similars, complements or opposites?
3. Which are higher and which lower? *

(A) Comparing the Soul Urge and Expression.
    1. Elements. (Consult the list on page 167.)
       Note whether you will meet with opposition and
       the consequent need for adjustment; whether

* This classification was contributed to Numerology by Mr. Clifford W. Cheasley.

the similarity will produce too much force, materialism or instability; or if the placid congeniality will tend to produce dullness and apathy.

2. Similars, complements and opposites.

If the numbers of Soul Urge and Expression are the same, there is danger of over-balance or negativity. If you can do exactly what you want to do, you will either *overdo* it or become so "fed-up" with it that the two positives produce the negative. The remedy in this case is to take the sum of the two numbers or their *Essence* for your constructive Expression.

If the two numbers are complements (i.e. both odd or both even), you will find satisfaction and harmony in the same *type* of desire and expression. (Always remember that 1, 6 and 22 are "dual.")

If the two numbers are opposites, you will meet with frustration. You would be constantly urged to create what you could not express.

3. Higher or Lower.

If the Soul Urge is higher than the Expression, you would have more ideas than you could use. If the Expression is higher, you would not have sufficient incentive to express your quota of ability.

(B) Comparing the Soul Urge and the Life Path.

1. Elements. Consult the list under "Elements" with a view to relating Desire and Opportunity.

2. Similars, complements and opposites.

If the Soul Urge and Life Path are similars, you will find your life running in an easy, happy groove. You will always have the chance to do what you want to do.

If they are complements, you will find more *growth* than in the former combination, for although you may do the *type* of thing you want to, there will be stimulation in the degrees of difference.

If they are opposites, you will have difficulty in finding the opportunity to express your real ideals.

3. Higher or Lower.

If the Soul Urge is higher, you will have to rise above your experiences or become their victim.

If the Life Path is higher, your experiences will become *requirements*.

(C) Comparing the Expression and the Life Path.

1. Elements. Consult the list under "Elements" with a view to relating Ability and Opportunity. If the two are congenial you will always find the work that you can do; if they are disciplinary or unadaptable, you will have to struggle to find a place for yourself.

2. Similars, complements and opposites.

If the Expression and Life Path are similars, this is the "Easiest Way." (Children named before birth will choose their own date.) On this Path you will have the opportunity for Self-Perfection.

If they are complements, you may meet with some difficulties, but none that are insurmountable. This is the most fortunate combination of all for it offers development, but no hardships.

If they are opposites, there will be much necessary adjustment and little real harmony. All the lessons will be new and none of them will be easy to learn.

3. Higher or Lower.

If the Expression is higher, you will contact people, situations and environment on a lower level of life. You will meet with nothing superior to yourself and will find your opportunities limited. On this Path you are the Teacher and Uplifter. If the Path is higher, you will be obliged to *climb* to meet your opportunities, but you will find awaiting you influential friends, superior conditions and *growth*.

ASSOCIATIONS

In the selection of associates Numerology is indispensable. If you are contemplating that highly important step in your life—Matrimony—you want to know all you can about the one you have selected as a life partner; but how many people *can* know very much about each other until they have spent a portion of their lives together? And even if you think you are thoroughly acquainted with his or her nature, abilities and ideals, how do you know whether you are going to pull *together* and if your separate lines of development will, in the future, run parallel or go off at tangents? At this point Numerology steps in and tells you all you need to know.

First of all, get the Chart. In all relationships that are to endure, the inner urges and inclinations, points of view and standards *must* harmonize; therefore, compare first the two Soul Urge numbers. Use the same general rules that you did in your own Chart. See if the elements are irreconcilable or capable of harmonization. See if the numbers are similars, complements or opposites. (Disregard the "Higher and Lower.")

If the two numbers are similars, there would be sure to be harmony, sympathy and understanding; you would both have the *same* method of approach toward *any* situation—but mightn't you become a little bored and static, eventually? Perhaps not, but there would be danger of it.

If the numbers are complements, you would have the same *type* of philosophy but would give to each other the necessary stimulus of differences.

If the numbers are *opposites,* abandon the idea of marriage altogether, for you would find irreconcilable antagonisms which would be likely to send you on the rocks. This latter is, of course, not always true. Many people are so subject to discipline that they can adjust themselves to any situation in life and learn to tolerate it. Most of the failures in marriage, however, can be attributed to the inability of the two involved to think alike or feel alike—or *understand* each other. "Where a man's heart is, there is his treasure also" and if you would remain the "treasure" of the one you have chosen, or continue to regard that one as your own treasure, look well at your Soul Numbers.

The Expression is of less importance in this relationship. It is rather better that the two should differ for the sake of variety.

Look next at the two Life Paths. Do your opportunities lie along entirely different lines—and shall you be able, if so, to follow them independently? If the Man has a Path of 5, shall you, the Woman, be resigned to frequent separation and bear patiently with his continual "moving about"? Will you give him the freedom demanded by his 5? Or, if the conditions are reversed, will he give you yours? If his Path is 2 or 4, shall you insist that he seek the job of 8, to satisfy your own ambition?

Do not overlook the Karmic Lessons. It is highly desirable that you be able to supply each others' "lacks" and help each other make up the lessons of past evasions.

Look next at your Cycles and Pinnacles (consult the Tables). Is this a propitious time to be married? Can you both safely assume new duties and responsibilities— *now?* or should you wait until the vibrations are more friendly to the relationship? If the Cycle or Pinnacle Number of either of you is 9, remember that 9 is the Finisher and not the Beginner and that life is liable to step in and cause your separation or the *termination* of the new venture.

Look next at your Personal Years. In addition to knowing that 9 finishes, we know that 3 and 5 *scatter,* and while they are excellent vibrations for pleasure and experimentation, they have few stabilizing qualities. If the year is 7, you will find personal and physical adjustments difficult; 7 prefers to be alone and is not given to demonstrations. What is "taken on" in the 1 Personal Year is usually *kept*—certainly for the duration of its own Cycle of 9 years; the 2 and 4 are enclosed and secure; the 6 is highly domestic and adjusting and therefore the *best* marriage vibration; the 8 brings strength and balance.

The Expression number of one on the Life Path number of the other brings the relationship of teacher to pupil. The pupil (Life Path) is apt to tire of it.

Follow these suggestions as to analysis and time and you will find yourself armed with counsel far superior to any your best friend could give you.

The choice of friends follows the same general rules, but they need not be so strictly related. Many lasting friendships are found with the *same* Soul Number—and indeed, that is usually the attraction. Daily contact is a test that few friendships are put to and partings and reunions only serve to fan the flame. If the Soul Numbers, however, are irreconcilable, there is every likelihood that the friendship will wane or die with the coming of a new Pinnacle influence.

Partners in business together should have the same Expression but differ in the Soul Urge. Here *opposites* may work together with fine results for while they will be *expressing* along the same lines, their dissimilarity in viewpoint will make for expansion in policy, and their different angles of sympathy and understanding will reach a larger group of people. Similarity in Soul Urge and Expression always produces a one-track result, and the business falls into a rut that only a new partner could destroy.

CITIES, TOWNS AND COUNTRIES

If you are unhappy or unsuccessful in the place where you are living and are free to make a choice as to where you shall go, examine carefully your own motives for making the change and ask yourself just what you want the new city, town or country to do for you.

If you want encouragement for your Soul Urge or want to establish yourself where people are doing the things that represent your idea of happiness and satisfaction, seek a place whose *Expression* is a similar or a complemental of your own Soul Number.

If you are looking for a market for your wares, seek the place that *wants* (Soul Urge) what you have to *give* (your Expression).

If you are looking for experience, the place which *expresses* your Life Path number will give it to you—but it may not give you an easy time, for the things you will encounter will be new.

———

Our own street and house numbers have a decided effect upon what we want to do or are trying to do. Try to relate your own Chart numbers to the numbers you are able to choose for yourself, and take on those that will help you to do what you want to do, what you can do and what you must do.

———

CHAPTER XIV

YOUR PAST, PRESENT AND FUTURE

The "Immediate Period" Table

EACH separate letter of your name carries its influence to your general make-up and equipment, as we have seen by the Inclusion Table and the Planes of Expression. Each letter, in addition to its place as a part of the whole, has its own special and *concentrated* influence at a certain definite *time* in your life—that is, during its own "transit." We "live through" each letter in turn, and the period of influence of each letter is determined by its number value *in terms of years*.

Thus, A, having the value of 1, has a "duration of influence" of 1 year; B of 2, C of 3, etc. In this way we may know exactly what vibrations we are contacting in *any* given year of our lives, whether in the past, now or in the future. We "live through" our entire first name, and then begin it again, carrying out the "Table" as far as we like. *Under* the first name we set the second and proceed in the same manner. Under the second we set the third, and if there are more than three, these also must be set down, one beneath the other.

This Table presents many intricacies and difficulties and several volumes could be written on this subject alone. You cannot expect to read and understand it *thoroughly* unless you are familiar not only with the meaning of every letter in the alphabet, but of every *combination* these letters make when appearing together.

This branch of Numerology is still in its infancy, but valuable contributions are being made continually by earnest students of the science and the results of their constant research and conclusions should be watched for with great interest. The best suggestion for the present is, Do what you can with the knowledge you have and you will be rewarded with many startling and interesting *facts* which will help you to check up on the past, guide you now and forearm you for the future. LEARN WHAT TO EXPECT.

A, J and S	endure in their influence for	1	Year,	for their value is	1.
B, K and T	" " " " "	2	Years,	" " " "	2.
C, L and U	" " " " "	3	"	" " " "	3.
D, M and V	" " " " "	4	"	" " " "	4.
E, N and W	" " " " "	5	"	" " " "	5.
F, O and X	" " " " "	6	"	" " " "	6.
G, P and Y	" " " " "	7	"	" " " "	7.
H, Q and Z	" " " " "	8	"	" " " "	8.
I and R	" " " " "	9	"	" " " "	9.

METHOD

Place the letters of your various names in a line across the paper—allowing the whole first line for the first name, the second line for the second, etc. Write each letter the same number of *times* as its duration in *years*, for each year of your life is to be considered separately.

Until one is familiar with this Table, it is best to *begin* with the year of birth, when the vibratory force of the *first* letter of each name is felt at the same time. The *initials* of the name are thus set up in a perpendicular column and the Table is then carried forward to the age desired or the age at present attained.

The order of arrangement is as follows:—

Age ....
First name ....
Second name ....
Other "middle" name (if any) ....
Last name ....
Essence of the letters ....

Personal Year ....
Universal Year ....
Calendar date ....

(It is advisable to leave a space between the "Essence" and the "Personal Year" because of a necessary "turn" after the birthday. Remember that your Personal Year is governed by the Calendar Year and has nothing to do with your birthday; it changes when the calendar year changes. Provide yourself with *block* paper, divided into small squares, in order that you may keep the divisions separated. Make a dash or division line as soon as each letter influence is terminated between that and the next letter; do the same with the Cycles of years from 1 to 9; this will facilitate the reading of the Table.)

Realize that when a child is born, although he immediately comes into the influence of the letters of his name, he is 0 years old, and will not be 1 year old until his next birthday, but he is *in* his first year; therefore a *turn* must be made from the division of Personal, Universal and Calendar Years to the division of Age, Names and Essence. This turn lasts until the new calendar year comes in, at which time we read *straight down* the line until the birthday, when another turn is made. These turns are made simply for clarity and convenience in keeping together the influences that are operating at the same time.

For example:—We will set up the Immediate Period Table of

Eva Amy Downs, born August 12th, 1920.

We now turn back to our "Order of Arrangement." On the first line *across* we write in the numbers that represent the age of Eva Amy Downs, beginning with 0 and extending the Table to any desired length, depending upon how far we want to look into her future.

Under the number 1 (her first year) we set the *initials*
                                                    E
of her name in a *perpendicular* column A. We then re-
                                                    D
turn to the first name-line and write E 4 times more— 5 in all—for E carries its influence for 5 years. We then write V 4 times (influence of 4 years) and A once (influence of 1 year). On the same line we begin the name EVA again and write as before, extending it as far as we have decided upon.

On the next line—the "Amy"-line—we do not write A again, for its influence is 1 year, but proceed to M and write it 4 times; then to Y and write it 7 times—carrying out the name AMY as far as we have gone with EVA.

On the next line we write 3 more D's, 6 O's, 5 W's, 5 N's, 1 S and repeat as desired.

On the next line we take the Essence * or sum of each *group* of letters in each perpendicular column, in order to learn what the sum total of the various vibrations is giving at the time.

We now proceed to the Year-division and write the results directly under the O of the age-line, because she had

---

* Much valuable information on the subject of the "Essence" has been contributed to numerology by Mr. C. A. Parcell.

a Personal Year as soon as she was born, and came into a certain Universal Year in a certain Calendar Year. We find that her Personal Year in the year of her birth was 5 (the *first* Personal Year is always the same as the Life Path number); that the Universal Year was 3 and that the date was 1920. We must make the "turn" at once, for the date and Universal Year had been in operation since January 1st and Eva May did not come upon the scene until August. After January 1st, 1921, we draw the line straight down and read it in a perpendicular column until her birthday in August, when we again make a turn, for as soon as she has had her first birthday, she is *in* her *second* year.

We have now completed the mechanics of her Immediate Period Table up to her 21st year, in the year 1941.

There is a common saying in Numerology, as in Astrology, that "Any fool can set up a Chart, but only a wise man can read it." Patience and accuracy are all that is needful to set up the Immediate Period Table, but knowledge and *experience* (especially the latter) are the absolute requisites for judging it.

We shall give a brief reading of the Table of Eva Amy Downs, based upon what you have already learned from Numerology.

We shall pre-suppose that her Chart has been carefully analyzed and that you are very well acquainted with her main vibrations and Planes of Expression.

She started life with two physical letters and one mental, a 1 Essence and a 5 Personal Year. The E (first vowel) would make her a very energetic baby and the A very active; D is not always good for health, but the Essence of these letters is 1 and the chances are that her

EVA AMY DOWNS

IMMEDIATE PERIOD TABLE

Age	0	1	2	3	4	5	6	7	8	9	10	11	12	13	14	15	16	17	18	19	20	21
Name		E	E	E	E	E	-V	V	V	V	-A	-E	E	E	E	E	-V	V	V	V	-A	-E
Name		A	-M	M	M	M	-Y	Y	Y	Y	Y	Y	Y	-A	-M	M	M	M	-Y	Y	Y	Y
Name		D	D	D	D	-O	O	O	O	O	O-	W	W	W	W	W	-N	N	N	N	N-	S-
Ess.		1	4	4	4	6	8	8	8	8	5	8	8	2	5	5	4	4	7	7	4	4
P.Y.	5	6	7	8	9	-1	2	3	4	5	6	7	8	9-	1	2	3	4	5	6	7	8
U.Y.	3	4	5	6	7	8	9	-1	2	3	4	5	6	7	8	9-	1	2	3	4	5	6
Cal.	20	21	22	23	24	25	26	27	28	29	30	31	32	33	34	35	36	37	38	39	40	41

first year of life would find her in sound health, except for the reactions of the storms and tempers of her scattering and willful 5-Year. After January, 1921, when her Personal Year is 6, we shall expect to find her more harmonious and amenable.

On her birthday in August, she picks up an M—another earth-vibration—giving her a 4-Essence. This gives her two letters that are lowering to the vitality and with the coming of her 7 Personal Year, her health will have to be carefully watched, for 7 is unfriendly to the physical body.

Between her 5th and 10th years her intuitional faculties will develop with amazing rapidity and she is liable to be considered a "strange" child. The Y (Intuitional-dual) will make her timid and uncertain about revealing her thoughts and she will be inclined to retire into herself and live her own life; the O, at the same time (Emotional-inspired) will be protective to the lack of balance in the Y and will clarify and inspire her imagination and intuition gained through the balanced V; the 8 Essence should give her the power to give brilliant expression to the pictures of her imagination.

When she comes into the A, after her 9th birthday, she will make an important change—probably a change in residence—and the months between August and December, 1929 will be full of change and activity for her (note the 5 Essence and her 5 Personal Year). In 1933 she completes a Life Cycle and the year will not be an easy one for her.

Because of the E in her Table she will be restless and full of inspiration; through the A she will meet another change in her life; the difficult, physical W will not lessen her trials and the emotional 2, as the Essence of the letters, will only increase her sensitivity, lower her vitality and promote an inclination to frequent tears. The 9 of her Personal Year will represent some loss or sacrifice for her, and altogether the period will be full of trial and unhappiness.

She will begin her love affairs early—certainly by the time she is 16, for she will be influenced by a return of her dreams and live in the imagination (in V), will still be under the physical M (a marriage letter), and will add to these vibrations the 5 of a new N which, although mental, is dual. The 4 of her Essence will not hold down the 3 of her Personal Year and she will seek pleasure and the society of new friends.

When she is 19 she will probably marry—although any Numerologist would advise her against it, for she will be under a Y (7) and also a 7 Essence—but her 6 Personal Year will turn her thoughts in that direction and the A in her Table, on her 19th birthday indicates another change of home, which she will want to be her own.

If you have already noted her principal numbers, you are not surprised to find her meeting many difficulties in life, for she is 7 in the Soul and 7 in Expression—both of which must be fitted to a 5–Path. Note her 11-Pinnacle.

This is but a brief analysis, leaving much unsaid, but giving you an indication of what you may already discover in your own Table, without the knowledge of the minute inter-relations of the numbers and letters. Do not attempt predictions; look only at the "high spots," relating them to the Personal Years in which they occur and *always* referring them to your present Cycle and Pinnacle. As regards the letters, depend upon your Table of the

Planes of Expression, for that will tell you whether the influences around you are mostly Mental, Physical, Emo‑tional or Intuitional. Watch for the changes in A.

Following is a general Table which may be helpful in noting *indications,* but must not be depended upon for absolute accuracy, since that can only be attained through a knowledge of the letters in *association* with each other.

Change and Activity—A, E-N-W, T (apt to mean a change of home).
Health—Lowered Vitality—B, D, M.
Emotions—I, R, S, U, X.
Love Affairs or Marriage—B, E-N-W, M, O, T and Z (some‑times).
Responsibility—F, J, O.
Secrecy—G, P, Y, Z.
Finances—G (gain), H (gain or strain), U (loss), N, Q.
Delay or Accidents—I, R.
Nerves—I, R, K.
Travel—A, D, L, M, O, V, W, X.

Much more might be added to this list, but would better be reserved for a more intensive study of the Table. A few points may be noted, however, in regard to the Essence and Personal Year.

If the Essence is the same as the Personal Year Num‑ber, they are liable to negativize each other. For ex‑ample:—

If both are 1—Over-activity, producing no results.
"   "   "   2—Tax on the health; possibility of poverty; dis‑appointment.
"   "   "   3—Scattering of the nerves and forces.
"   "   "   4—No let-up from confining work; limitation.
"   "   "   ·5—Misuse of freedom. "Satan will find mischief," etc.
"   "   "   6—Too much home and family; taxed with respon‑sibility.
"   "   "   7—Too introspective; no opportunity for advance‑ment.

If both are 8—Physical and financial strain.
  "   "   " 9—Emotional strain; sacrifice.
  "   "   " 11—Overstrained nerves; overtaxed brain.
  "   "   " 22—Danger of shock.

In reading the Essence alone, judge it largely by its own number-significance.

The Personal Year begins to operate in *full force* when the 1 Personal *Month* is reached; it begins, however, on January 1st. If a 1 Personal Year falls in the middle of a letter-Cycle, the indicated change will be most effective after the letter-Cycle has terminated.

The most important changes in the life occur in the 1, 5 and 9 Personal Years. A 7 or a 9 Personal Year usually means loss. 8 and 9 are the most *expressive* years —8 materially, 9 emotionally.

The vibration of each month is most active between the 5th and 25th.

Soul Urge, Expression, Life Path, Karmic Lessons and Challenge have added importance and significance when the Personal Year is the same number.

ALWAYS LOOK AT CYCLES AND PINNACLES when reading this Table.

SUMMARY OF THE OPERATIONS
Complete Chart of HENRY FORD—born July 30th, 1863.

241

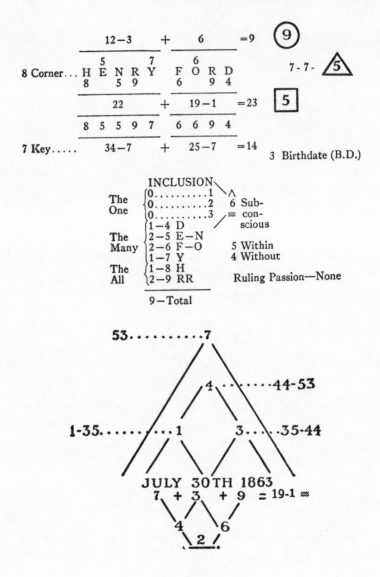

PLANES OF EXPRESSION

	MENTAL	PHYSICAL	EMOTIONAL	INTUITIONAL
Inspired		E	ORR	=4 Inspired
Dual	HN			FY =4 Dual
Balanced		D		=1 Balanced
	2	2	3	2

Soul Urge— 9
Quiescent— 5
Expression—5
Birthdate— 3
Life Path— 1

The ONE— None
The MANY—6
The ALL— 3

"Within" (Inspirational)—5
"Without" (Practical) —4
Cornerstone—8
Key Number—7
1st Vowel—E
Eccentric Angle—1

ELEMENTS
Fire— 2/9
Earth—3/9
Air— 3/9
Water—1/9

PLANES OF EXPRESSION
Mental— 2/9
Physical— 2/9
Emotional— 3/9
Intuitional—2/9

Inspired— 4/9
Dual— 4/9
Balanced—1/9

COLORS
Soul—Yellow gold
Q.S.—Turquoise
Expr.—Turquoise
Life Path—Red

GEMS
Soul—Opals
Q.S.—Turquoise
Expr.—Turquoise
Life Path—Rubies

MUSICAL TONES
Soul—All Tones
Q.S.—G
Expr.—G
Life Path—C

IMMEDIATE PERIOD TABLE

Age	65	66	67	68	69	70
1st Name	Y	Y	Y	Y —	H	H
Last Name	R	R	R	R	R	R
Essence	7	7	7	7	8	8
Personal Year	3	4	5	6	7	8
Universal Year	2	3	4	5	6	7
Calendar Date	1928	1929	1930	1931	1932	1933

In 1931—

Personal Year—6
Present Cycle—9
Present Pinnacle—7
Age Next Birthday—68

A FINAL WORD

In the Egyptian Ritual of the Dead (called the *Book of the Master of the Secret House*), the Indian *Vedas*, the Chinese *Circle of the Heavens* and the Hebrew *Kabbala* we may find *records* to prove that the Science of Number was in use over 11,000 years ago. There is good *evidence* that it is more than twice as old as that.

We know that it was taught to Moses as an Egyptian Priest and brought by him to the Hebrews. Other Priests spread it to the Chaldeans, Phoenicians, Chinese and Hindus. Pythagoras, after spending twenty-two years in the East, brought it to the Greeks.

Pythagoras, the "Father of Number" lived in the 6th century, B. C. He is responsible for the foundation upon which the greatest philosophers have built their beliefs. He propounded the Theory of Sound, the Slant of the Zodiacal Circle, the Sun as the center of the Universe, the 47th problem of Euclid, the diatonic scale—and Numerology. He based his teachings upon Mathematics, Music and Astronomy, which he considered the "Triangular Foundation" of all the arts and sciences. Mathematics he held to be the first, for he affirmed that mathematics could exist without the other two, but that *nothing* could exist without Number.

The world is rapidly returning to the "Ancient Wisdom" and science is beginning to look beyond its facts and form for the "truth behind the veil." Many physicians today are using the harmonization of Sound and Color in the treatment of disease—with remarkable results.

It was encouraging to note a news item that appeared in the New York Herald-Tribune for November 25th, 1930, stating that a resolution had been adopted by the Academy of Medicine at its National Conference in New York to standardize the nomenclature of diseases by the use of *numbers!*

Perhaps that is only a short step to teaching them all what the numbers mean, and then indeed we shall all be in sight of the Promised Land—where every man knows himself and either loves or tolerates his neighbor.

Florence Campbell, M.A.

ANOTHER FINAL WORD

This fundamental text book on Number has gone through many editions since its first publication in 1931, without revisions or additions. Much has been discovered in this valuable field during the past twenty years through study and research—and vastly more through application to the individuals who have sought its counsel and students who have tested and found useful new angles of interpretation. These must await a newer and more enlarged edition.

There was from the start, however, a serious omission. The author, having been an astrologer long before her introduction to Number, wanted to include the correlations of the two with the original text. This was ruled against by the publishers, who wanted a book on Number alone.

Now that the opportunity has come to send the book forth again, we take this occasion to stress the importance of the close partnership. *Alone,* neither your stars nor your numbers tell the whole story about yourself, but each one opens the door of the other to fuller understanding and enlightenment. A brief list of the correlations will help you to compare your planets by sign, house and aspect with the numbers they represent according to their position in your charted Name and Birthdate. A weak Moon, for example, is strengthened by number 8 or 10 in the Soul Urge (its corollary), or a well-aspected Saturn will mitigate the difficulties of the karmic numbers.

The Soul Urge has its astrological correspondence in the *Moon*

The Ability in the *Ascendant*	The Key in *Jupiter*
The Life Path in the *Sun*	The Karmic Lessons in *Saturn*
The Cornerstone in *Mercury*	The Challenge in *Uranus*
The First Vowel in *Venus*	The Quiescent Self in *Neptune*
The Birthday Number in *Mars*	

(The true place of PLUTO has not been agreed upon—either in horoscopes or numberscopes)

"God always speaks twice." Through stars and numbers He speaks to us of the truths we need to know about ourselves—and all others.

FLORENCE EVYLINN CAMPBELL, M.A.